ADS:
Design & Make
Your Own

ADS!

Design & Make
Your Own

Abraham Switkin

 VAN NOSTRAND REINHOLD COMPANY
New York Cincinnati Toronto London Melbourne

For Daniel and Jill

Copyright © 1981 by Van Nostrand Reinhold Company
Library of Congress Catalog Card Number 80-18229
ISBN 0-442-24342-1

Printed in the United States of America.

Designed by Joel Weltman and Garabed Kasparian

Published by Van Nostrand Reinhold Company
135 West 50th Street
New York, NY 10020

Van Nostrand Reinhold Limited
1410 Birchmount Road
Scarborough, Ontario M1P 2E7, Canada

Van Nostrand Reinhold Australia Pty. Ltd.
17 Queen Street
Mitcham, Victoria 3132, Australia

Van Nostrand Reinhold Company Limited
Molly Millars Lane
Workingham, Berkshire, England

16 15 14 13 12 11 10 9 8 7 6 5 4 3 2

Library of Congress Cataloging in Publication Data

Switkin, Abraham.
    How to design and make your own ads.
    Includes index.
    1.   Advertising — Handbooks, manuals, etc.
2.   Small business — Handbooks, manuals, etc.
I.   Title.
HF5823.S96   659.1′02′02   80-18229
ISBN 0-442-24342-1

It is evident that today advertising is a necessity for any business person with a product or service to sell. In 1980, businesses chose to spend the awesome sum of $54.8 billion on media advertising alone.

Competition for the consumer's dollar has been fierce, resulting in the relentless pursuit of the consumer into every nook and cranny of his or her life. In 1980 the consumer found $15.6 billion worth of advertising in the newspapers he scanned, $3.2 billion in the magazines he read, $11.3 billion on the TV programs he watched, $3.7 million on the radio programs he listened to, $610 thousand on the streets and highways he traveled, and $7.7 billion in his mailbox.

Thus, in trying to capture the attention of the consumer, the small independent business person is fighting against tremendous odds. His potential customers are ad-weary and skeptical. His competition is strong. His overhead is high. His budget is strained. He lacks the savvy and the production facilities of the Madison Avenue ad agency. He can easily be reduced to a voice lost in the wilderness.

This book will help the small independent business person to reduce some of these difficulties and increase income.

The author, with forty-five years' experience as an advertising craftsman, art director, and teacher, willingly shares his knowledge of effective advertising. The tools and techniques necessary for the design and preparation of professional ads are presented in an easy-to-follow, practical, "how-to" guide for the nonprofessional.

No previous knowledge of advertising principles or methods is necessary. You must only know in advance what you want to sell. An understanding of your competition and your marketplace would, of course, be valuable.

Armed with the determination to compete, with a willingness to learn, and with less than $50.00 for supplies, the seller of virtually any product or service can (really!) produce a very inexpensive, yet profitable, ad, series of ads, or advertising campaign.

This book is intended to be read from beginning to end, chapter by chapter, by those who wish to develop an ad from the initial idea to the final production stage. Specialists, such as graphic designers, copy writers, illustrators, or others who need only to supplement an existing base of knowledge, however, may read chapters individually as required.

In Chapter 1, An Ad is Born, an introductory overview of the various steps in the development of an ad are presented and illustrated.

Chapter 2, The Media, addresses the problem of choosing the most appropriate advertising medium. The nature and advantages of newspapers, magazines, theater programs, outdoor displays, directories, window displays, nine forms of direct advertising, and transit advertising are explored.

Once the advertising medium is chosen, the content of the ad must be developed. In Chapter 3, The Copy, help is provided for writing dramatic and effective headlines and subheads. The principles of copy writing and the different types of copy are identified.

Chapter 4, The Type, aids in selecting and ordering the most suitable type styles for the written copy. Two simplified alternatives to type setting are described for the layman who may want to consider preparing his own hand lettering.

Illustrations are often a necessary adjunct to straight copy. In Chapter 5, the purposes and types of various illustrations are discussed. These can be copied directly from this book to save time and money. Sources for obtaining additional illustrations are listed.

With the copy and illustrations prepared, the advertiser must arrange them so as to best attract and hold the potential buyer's attention. A step-by-step procedure for preparing a layout according to basic principles of advertising design is detailed in Chapter 6, The Layout.

In Chapter, 7, The Pasteup, specific directions for final preparation of the layout are provided. Topics covered include making mechanicals and photostats; ordering and using colored tints, shading film, and overlays; and understanding halftone and combination plates. A checklist is given to insure the absence of any errors in the final preparation of the layout.

David John Switkin

Acknowledgments

This book came about with the help of many people. Colleagues, friends, and professional associates have willingly shared their energies and talents. Because of the author's death prior to publication, an all-inclusive list for this tribute is not available. Gratitude and pride must substitute for any printed citation.

A special thanks to two special people: Anne Switkin, the author's wife, provided the love and encouragement necessary for an undertaking of this magnitude; Bob Esposito, an outstanding graphics professional and indeed a true friend, prepared the majority of the illustrations, often under very difficult circumstances but always with care and fidelity.

To the extent that this book serves its purpose, i.e., to aid the small business man or woman, the credit belongs to the author, Abraham Switkin. For any inaccuracies or inconsistencies, I must take sole blame. As the author's son, I undertook as a labor of love the author's responsibilities in the final preparation of this book. I am grateful to have had this opportunity.

David J. Switkin

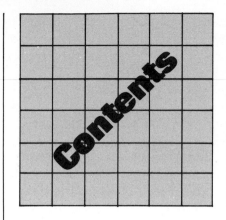

Contents

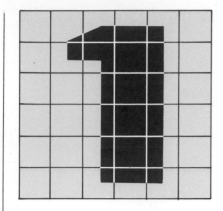

AN AD IS BORN

The development of an actual
advertisement from start to finish

An advertisement does not just happen. It comes about as a result of the combined efforts of a group of people who each specialize in a particular part of the job.

They pool their expertise under the guidance of an art director, and, thus, another ad is born.

You are going to substitute for all those people, except, of course, in the making of the plate and the actual printing. If this sounds formidable, let me assure you that it really is not. Given a few guidelines, you are capable of doing a very adequate job of developing an ad to the point of printing.

Nine steps (right) are necessary to arrive at a finished ad. After you have decided what kind of ad you want, there are just five steps to develop it. These are indicated by asterisks, and each step is presented on the following pages.

1 Business man or woman decides to advertise

2 Select the media

3 Write the copy*

4 Design the ad*

5 Order the type*

6 Obtain the illustration*

7 Make the pasteup*

8 Make the plate

9 Do the printing

THE CASE HISTORY OF A NEWSPAPER AD

STEP 1 Business man or woman decides to advertise

STEP 2 Select the media

STEP 3 Write the copy*

The Order Form with Full Copy

LOIS HOLLAND CALLAWAY INC.

Work Requisition

Pertinent Information:

Client OTB

OTB has requested that we prepare a 250 ad which will let the fans know that starting Monday they can see the last ½ mile of the 7th race (triple) from Yonkers. The ad is scheduled to run Mon. Aug. 23 in the N.Y. News, Post, and Daily Racing Form
Layout and copy are needed ASAP, this pm if at all possible.

COPY AS FOLLOWS:

SEE THE FINISH OF A YONKERS BIG TRIPLE EVERY WEEKNIGHT ON CHANNEL 5

MONDAY THROUGH THURSDAY, YOU CAN SEE THE LAST HALF MILE OF THE BIG TRIPLE 7th RACE FROM YONKERS (ON FRIDAYS IT'S THE 3rd RACE). IF YOU TUNE IN TO "THE 10 O'CLOCK NEWS" BETWEEN 10:30 and 11:00 P.M. SO GET SOME ACTION WITH OTB THAT DAY AND SEE THE ACTION THAT NIGHT ON CHANNEL 5

LOGO INCLUDED

Breakdown of Copy into Units

10

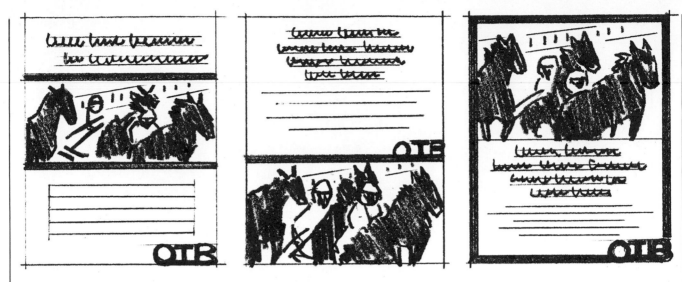

Thumbnail sketches are made.

STEP
4 **Design the ad***

Full-size rough sketch is made.

See the finish of a Yonkers big Triple every weeknight on Channel 5.

The heading, to exact size and style, is ordered from the typographer.

Monday through Thursday,
you can see the last half mile of the big Triple 7th race
from Yonkers (on Fridays it's the 3rd race)
if you tune in to "The 10 O'clock News" between 10:30 and 11:00 pm.
So get some action with OTB that day
and see the action that night
on Channel 5.

The minor copy is also ordered to specifications.

STEP 5 **Order the type***

A photostat copy of the existing logo is made to the size required.

STEP 6 **Obtain the illustration***

The illustration is rendered.

All units are assembled in exact position according to the final layout sketch. This *mechanical* goes to the photoengraver to be converted to a plate for actual printing.

STEP 7 **Make the pasteup***

STEP 8 **Make the plate**

STEP 9 **Do the printing**

THE TOOLS AND MATERIALS
FOR DESIGN AND LAYOUT WORK

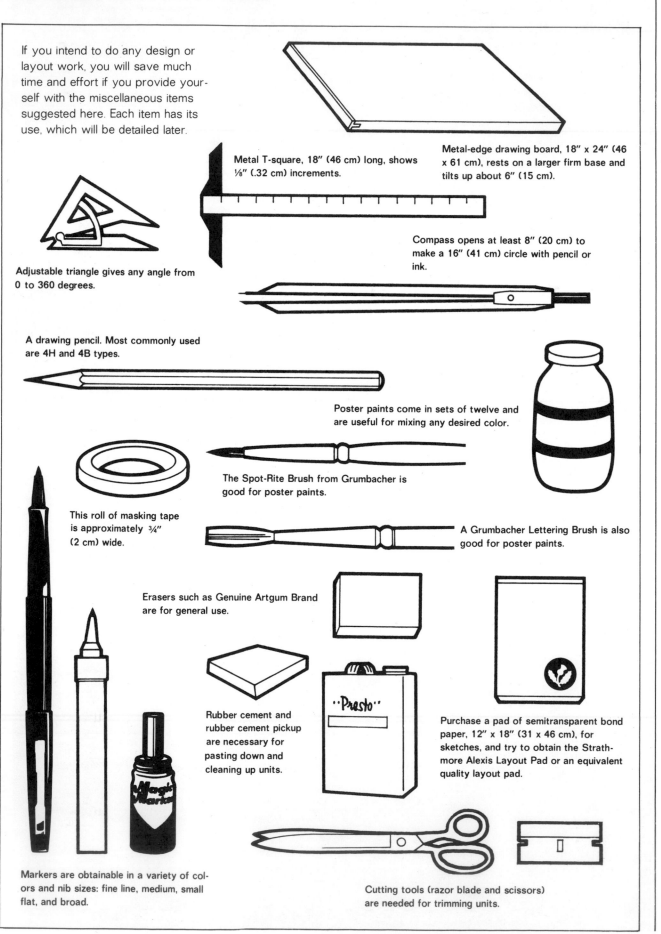

If you intend to do any design or layout work, you will save much time and effort if you provide yourself with the miscellaneous items suggested here. Each item has its use, which will be detailed later.

Metal T-square, 18″ (46 cm) long, shows ⅛″ (.32 cm) increments.

Metal-edge drawing board, 18″ x 24″ (46 x 61 cm), rests on a larger firm base and tilts up about 6″ (15 cm).

Adjustable triangle gives any angle from 0 to 360 degrees.

Compass opens at least 8″ (20 cm) to make a 16″ (41 cm) circle with pencil or ink.

A drawing pencil. Most commonly used are 4H and 4B types.

Poster paints come in sets of twelve and are useful for mixing any desired color.

The Spot-Rite Brush from Grumbacher is good for poster paints.

This roll of masking tape is approximately ¾″ (2 cm) wide.

A Grumbacher Lettering Brush is also good for poster paints.

Erasers such as Genuine Artgum Brand are for general use.

Rubber cement and rubber cement pickup are necessary for pasting down and cleaning up units.

Purchase a pad of semitransparent bond paper, 12″ x 18″ (31 x 46 cm), for sketches, and try to obtain the Strathmore Alexis Layout Pad or an equivalent quality layout pad.

Markers are obtainable in a variety of colors and nib sizes: fine line, medium, small flat, and broad.

Cutting tools (razor blade and scissors) are needed for trimming units.

THE MEDIA

The advantages and limitations of advertising media and how to choose the best one for your needs

THE MEDIA

There are various media through which a manufacturer or merchant can advertise his message before the public. The major problems of the advertiser are to select the right medium that will reach the desired group of people and to prepare the advertisement so that it will be most effective in that particular medium.

The more important media may be classified as follows:
Periodical advertising
Mass advertising
Direct advertising

The periodical media discussed in this chapter include newspapers, magazines, directories, and programs.

NEWSPAPERS

There are about 1,600 daily newspapers and about 400 weekly newspapers published in the United States. Of the daily papers about one-fifth are morning papers and four-fifths are evening papers. There are also about 600 Sunday papers published regularly. Among these daily, weekly, and Sunday newspapers are some foreign language, business, and financial newspapers. In the United States approximately 62,000,000 copies of daily newspapers are sold each day, and approximately 53,000,000 copies of Sunday papers are sold each week.

Many of the metropolitan daily and Sunday papers have an enormous circulation, not only in the home cities but also in all the cities and towns for hundreds of miles around. For example, Boston papers circulate in all parts of New England except southern and western Connecticut; the publisher of one New York Sunday paper claims a circulation of more than 11,000 copies in Ohio, which is more than 400 miles distant.

The following list gives the recent (July 1980) circulation of some of the largest newspapers published in the United States.

Daily Circulation

Atlanta, Georgia	
Journal Constitution	436,263
Baltimore, Maryland	
News-American	151,000
Boston, Massachusetts	
The Globe	515,000
Times	1,024,322
New Orleans, Louisiana	
Times-Picayune	285,000
New York, New York	
Times	914,938
Daily News	1,386,095
Wall Street Journal	1,798,416

Newspaper Readership

These daily circulation figures indicate how universally the newspaper is read. They also suggest the varied character of the readers. Rich and poor, old and young, men and women: all read the newspaper. Because of

the wide variety of interests of its readers, the newspaper is best adapted to advertising those commodities that are in more or less general use. When the commodities are of interest to a very limited group of people, newspaper advertising is not advisable because so small a percentage of its readers would be potential buyers. Other forms of advertising are likely to be more productive for goods that appeal only to special groups.

The advertiser must therefore consider whether the readers of a particular newspaper are prospects for the purchase of his commodity. The class of readers is determined to a certain extent by the character of the news and editorials. Papers featuring extremely sensational news are naturally read by a group of people totally different from the readers of more conservative papers.

There is so much print in a newspaper that the average reader can read only a small part thoroughly. The advertiser must realize that, unless especially attractive features are used in the ad, it will suffer in the competition for attention. His message must be told in a concise and attractive way that will make an impression even when the advertisement is merely scanned.

Advertising Rates

In general, the cost of advertising space depends on the circulation, or on the number and character of the people whom the advertisement is likely to reach. Newspapers make available to advertisers reports concerning their circulation. In the past because of differences in the methods of reporting numbers of sample copies and unsold papers returned from news dealers, there was often much doubt concerning circulation figures quoted by newspaper publishers. Nearly all reputable publishers now have their circulation data audited and attested to by the Audit Bureau of Circulations. In this way the advertiser is assured that the circulation claims of publishers are true. Circulation now means actual net paid circulation.

Advantages of Newspaper Advertising

The newspaper offers the following advantages as an advertising medium:

1. The newspaper is widely read.

2. Its circulation is localized. It is, therefore, the natural advertising medium of retail stores and can be used as a means of cooperating with a manufacturer in an intensive sales campaign.

3. The newspaper furnishes an excellent medium for tryout campaigns.

4. It is a medium for obtaining quick sales.

5. The appeal may be made very timely.

6. The copy may be changed daily.

7. Planning long in advance is not necessary. Although the copy may be submitted late at night, the newspaper containing the advertisement will be on the breakfast table the next morning.

Display Advertising

There are two distinct divisions of newspaper advertising: display and classified. Display advertising is subdivided into local and national (sometimes called foreign) advertising.

On the average, about two-thirds of the advertising in the daily paper is local: display advertising of retail stores and classified advertising. One-third of the advertising is national: nationwide sales campaigns of manufacturers or producers.

A newspaper display ad.

Newspapers are geared to local advertising campaigns from which quick results are desired. The *Chicago Tribune* points out that advertising instituted in thirteen metropolitan distributing centers reaches a majority of the buyers of the country. Localized sales campaigns can be organized in one or many of these districts to supplement the advertising. Quick results over a large territory are thus obtained, and the circle around each center can later be enlarged.

The newspaper is the all-important advertising medium of the retail store. An examination of the daily newspaper advertising of any large city will show that without department-store advertising, the paper would be a financial failure. The local character of the newspaper and the possibility of a quick return from advertising make the paper the ideal medium for these merchants.

Classified Advertising

Classified advertising is grouped in designated sections of the paper according to category, for example, Help Wanted, Real Estate, and Lost and Found. The rate for classified advertisements is less than that for display advertising, and they are a convenience to the reader and a saving to the advertiser. The reader who is looking for a particular kind of advertisement will find groupings of ads in the category that interests him. The advertiser may, on this account, use a very small advertisement that would be lost if it were placed among larger ones.

In comparison with other advertisements, it is evident that the reader approaches classified advertisements in a different frame of mind. He turns to a page of classified advertisements to search for the particular advertisement that will meet his needs. Since his attention is voluntary, the advertiser does not need to rely to much extent on attention-getting display type styles to arouse the reader's interest.

Newspaper Space

Most newspaper pages are made up of eight columns, each column being about 2⅛ inches (5 cm) wide and containing about 295 agate (fourteen-to-the-inch) lines. The average page, therefore, contains something over 2,300 lines. The advertising-rate card of a newspaper gives the exact dimensions and also specifies any restrictions that there may be on the size of advertisements. Some papers refuse to accept an advertisement extending over two or more columns unless it contains at least a specified number of lines. For example, the paper may not accept an advertisement three columns wide unless it is at least fifty lines deep.

The advertising rates of newspapers are usually quoted per agate line. The advertiser is interested, however, in knowing how much he will get for his money; that is, how many people will have the opportunity of seeing his advertisement if he purchases space in a given newspaper. The relation between these two factors — rate per agate line and circulation — determines his actual cost. To determine a single cost figure that can be compared with similar figures for other newspapers, these factors may be combined to show what would be the cost of reaching

---

Stores, Miscellaneous   **3438**

SHOE STORE FOR SALE

With or without stock. Downtown Flushing area. Will sell as is or rent for other business. 266-0940 Mr. Cohen

VARIETY DISCOUNT STORE. Available for quick sale, excellent location. Church Ave cor Ocean Ave Bklyn. Call 462-2578.
8 to 12 AM Mon. thru Sat.

FOR SALE RECORD & BOOK STORE In immaculate cond. AAA location in N.J. Ideal for son or yourself. Fully stocked. Price stock & fixt. at cost. No goodwill. 201-568-0218 after 8PM.

Garages & Gas Stations   **3446**

GARAGE FLOORS
AVAILABLE
West 77th St. Area
Reasonable Rent
Call Mr. Sider, 799-3202

FAIRFIELD, CONNECTICUT
Huge gas station/garage-12 pumps, 12 lifts, 3 million gals; general repair & other related business. Tenant Income of $24,000. 1½ acres-$1,500,000. Call Art Overfield (203)255-3513.
FAIRFIELD COUNTY REAL ESTATE

A classified ad section.

AUTOMOBILE EXCHANGE
Selling your car? To place your ad call OX 5-3311

BUSINESS OPPORTUNITIES
3400

SITUATIONS WANTED
-3000-

AUCTION SALES
FURNITURE MACHINERY MERCHANDISE

ROOMS
—1900—

EMPLOYMENT AGENCIES
2500

DOGS, CATS AND OTHER PETS
3900

GOING OUT
Luncheon, Dinner, Dancing Suggestions

FARMS — COUNTRY HOMES
200

BUSINESS & INDUSTRIAL PROPERTIES
—800-1300—

Cooperative Apartments- Condominiums
1700

VACATION— LEISURE HOMES
-500-

SALES AND RENTALS
At the seashore . . . .
by the lake . . . .
in the mountains.

VACATION— LEISURE HOMES

Apartments, Cottages, Chalets, Hunting Cabins, Houses, Ski Lodges.

-500-

WANTED TO PURCHASE
-3300-

AUCTION SALES
FURNITURE MACHINERY MERCHANDISE

Southern Real Estate
300

Here are some of the classified advertising sections listed in the *New York Times* in a given week.

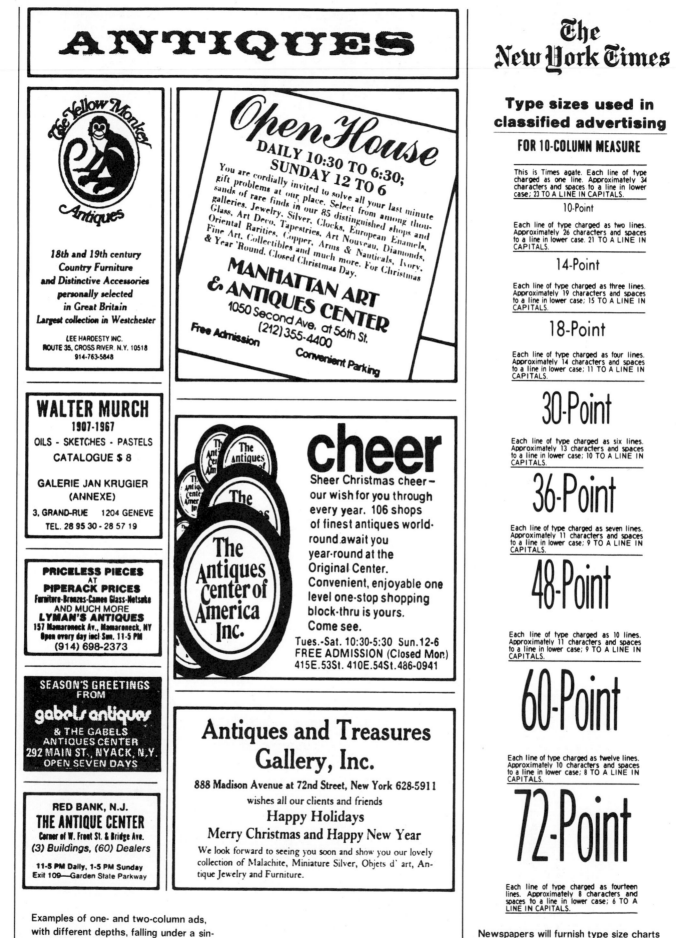

ANTIQUES

The Yellow Monkey Antiques

18th and 19th century
Country Furniture
and Distinctive Accessories
personally selected
in Great Britain
Largest collection in Westchester

LEE HARDESTY INC.
ROUTE 35, CROSS RIVER, N.Y. 10518
914-763-5848

Open House

DAILY 10:30 TO 6:30;
SUNDAY 12 TO 6

You are cordially invited to solve all your last minute gift problems at our place. Select from among thousands of rare finds in our 85 distinguished shops and galleries. Jewelry, Silver, Clocks, European Enamels, Glass, Art Deco, Tapestries, Art Nouveau, Diamonds, Oriental Rarities, Copper, Arms & Nauticals, Ivory, Fine Art, Collectibles and much more. For Christmas & Year 'Round. Closed Christmas Day.

MANHATTAN ART & ANTIQUES CENTER

1050 Second Ave. at 56th St.
(212) 355-4400

Free Admission   Convenient Parking

WALTER MURCH
1907-1967
OILS - SKETCHES - PASTELS
CATALOGUE $ 8

GALERIE JAN KRUGIER
(ANNEXE)

3, GRAND-RUE   1204 GENEVE
TEL. 28 95 30 - 28 57 19

cheer

Sheer Christmas cheer—
our wish for you through
every year. 106 shops
of finest antiques world-
round await you
year-round at the
Original Center.
Convenient, enjoyable one
level one-stop shopping
block-thru is yours.
Come see.

Tues.-Sat. 10:30-5:30 Sun. 12-6
FREE ADMISSION (Closed Mon.)
415E.53St. 410E.54St. 486-0941

The Antiques Center of America Inc.

PRICELESS PIECES
AT
PIPERACK PRICES
Furniture-Bronzes-Cameo Glass-Netsuke
AND MUCH MORE
LYMAN'S ANTIQUES
157 Mamaroneck Av., Mamaroneck, NY
Open every day incl Sun. 11-5 PM
(914) 698-2373

SEASON'S GREETINGS FROM
gabels antiques
& THE GABELS
ANTIQUES CENTER
292 MAIN ST., NYACK, N.Y.
OPEN SEVEN DAYS

RED BANK, N.J.
THE ANTIQUE CENTER
Corner of W. Front St. & Bridge Ave.
(3) Buildings, (60) Dealers

11-5 PM Daily, 1-5 PM Sunday
Exit 109—Garden State Parkway

Antiques and Treasures Gallery, Inc.

888 Madison Avenue at 72nd Street, New York 628-5911

wishes all our clients and friends
Happy Holidays
Merry Christmas and Happy New Year

We look forward to seeing you soon and show you our lovely collection of Malachite, Miniature Silver, Objets d'art, Antique Jewelry and Furniture.

Examples of one- and two-column ads, with different depths, falling under a single classified heading. Note the inclusion of local (New York), national, and even international advertisers.

The New York Times

Type sizes used in classified advertising

FOR 10-COLUMN MEASURE

This is Times agate. Each line of type charged as one line. Approximately 34 characters and spaces to a line in lower case; 23 TO A LINE IN CAPITALS.

10-Point

Each line of type charged as two lines. Approximately 26 characters and spaces to a line in lower case. 21 TO A LINE IN CAPITALS.

14-Point

Each line of type charged as three lines. Approximately 19 characters and spaces to a line in lower case; 15 TO A LINE IN CAPITALS.

18-Point

Each line of type charged as four lines. Approximately 14 characters and spaces to a line in lower case; 11 TO A LINE IN CAPITALS.

30-Point

Each line of type charged as six lines. Approximately 13 characters and spaces to a line in lower case; 10 TO A LINE IN CAPITALS.

36-Point

Each line of type charged as seven lines. Approximately 11 characters and spaces to a line in lower case; 9 TO A LINE IN CAPITALS.

48-Point

Each line of type charged as 10 lines. Approximately 11 characters and spaces to a line in lower case; 9 TO A LINE IN CAPITALS.

60-Point

Each line of type charged as twelve lines. Approximately 10 characters and spaces to a line in lower case; 8 TO A LINE IN CAPITALS.

72-Point

Each line of type charged as fourteen lines. Approximately 8 characters and spaces to a line in lower case; 6 TO A LINE IN CAPITALS.

Newspapers will furnish type size charts and rate cards upon request. Rates and dimensions will differ among papers, even within one locality.

No. 88 issued December 1, 1976, effective January 1, 1977

NYT The New York Times

Published every morning
Times Square, New York, N.Y. 10036

CLASSIFIED
ADVERTISING
RATES

Classification Index

one million people with one agate line. The resulting figure is called the *milline rate*. It may be found by the following formula:

$$\text{Milline Rate} = \frac{\text{Line Rate} \times 1,000,000}{\text{Circulation}}$$

Preferred Positions

An advertisement that is submitted with no stipulation made for its placement in the paper is given run-of-paper (R.O.P.) position. There are certain positions in the paper, however, where advertisements are more likely to be seen than in other places. Since these preferred positions are more valuable to advertisers, the publisher charges more for them. The additional charges for the various preferred positions differ greatly. For some positions the cost is twice or three times the ordinary base rate.

Some preferred positions are:
- Outside pages
- Special news pages (page two or three)
- Sports page
- Woman's page
- Amusement page
- Top of a column
- Top of a column next to reading matter
- Next to or following reading matter
- Next to and following reading matter

By developing certain special sections or pages, newspaper publishers have attempted to assure the advertiser that his display will not be overlooked by prospective consumers. Sports, household, financial, real-estate, textile, and hardware pages have been made interesting by articles and news items in these special fields. Advertisements allied to these subjects are likely to be seen by the desired group of readers when they are placed on these pages. Hence the advertiser is willing to pay an extra price for any of these preferred positions.

MAGAZINES

A wide variety of magazines, catering to the different interests and tastes of the public, are published in millions of copies every month. These magazines may be classified as follows:

General

Class

Trade, technical, and professional

Some of these magazines are published weekly, others every two weeks or monthly, and a few quarterly. Most magazines are sold and delivered on an annual subscription basis by mail, and single copies are sold from newsstands.

The Audit Bureau of Circulations lists 360 general magazines, 45 farm publications, 245 business publications, 215 religious publications, and numerous college papers.

Most magazines circulate widely throughout the United States and for that reason are suitable for national advertising. National advertising, however, presupposes that the advertiser has a sales organization competent to cover the whole country. If the advertiser does not have such an organization, he does not get the full benefit of the service for which he is paying.

A manufacturer or a merchant is not ready for national advertising until he has established production facilities and a sales organization adequate for handling nationwide sales.

There are about 200 magazines in America with circulations of more than 250,000.

General Magazines

The general magazine contains articles of interest to all groups of people. Some articles are on more or less technical subjects but are written in a popular style. The character of the reading matter indicates that these magazines are read by the general public and that they are excellent mediums for advertising products that are in general demand or for which a general demand may be stimulated.

An ad from *Cue*, a general magazine.

Some general magazines feature reading matter that appeals to persons with special interests in addition to containing articles of interest to all kinds of people. The specialized nature of the articles attracts a group of readers who, because of their interests, are considered to be natural prospects by the advertiser. Women's magazines, such as *Good Housekeeping*, *Vogue*, and *Ladies' Home Journal*, are in this group.

Class Magazines

Class magazines include sportsmen's magazines, religious papers, automobilists' journals, farm magazines, and the like. Such magazines reach a very select group for the advertiser of a specialized product.

An ad from the *American Music Teacher*, a class magazine.

Such magazines as *Automation*, *Farm Journal*, the *Christian Herald*, and *Field and Stream* are examples of class magazines. Since a magazine of this kind usually enjoys, to a great degree, the confidence of its particular readers, its prestige is shared by the advertiser. On this account and because of the homogeneous nature of the readers, the prices charged for advertising are often high.

Field and Stream, for example, with a circulation of 2,000,000, charges $16,600 for a black-and-white (b/w) page of advertising. This makes the cost per thousand readers $8.30 while the cost for some general magazines can fall within a $4-to-$6 range.

Farm publications make up an important part of this group of magazines. A large percentage of the population of the United States lives in rural communities. The buying power of this great rural population cannot be overlooked, and the surest way to reach a large part of the group is through farm publications. Often, these are read from cover to cover with loyalty and trustfulness.

Trade, Technical, and Professional Magazines

Trade, technical, and professional magazines are those publications that appeal to certain special groups. These include magazines for merchants of wool, hardware, or dry goods; for railroad workers, plumbers, or engineers; and for professionals such as doctors, teachers, or lawyers. Almost every department of business has its trade magazine. *Iron Age*,

An ad from *The Writer*, a trade magazine.

Beauty Trade, Hardware Age, Golf Digest, American Artist, Industry Week, Consumer Reports, Railroad, and an endless number of other magazines belong to this class. Although the price of advertising space may be high when compared to circulation, there is so little waste that the magazine may be the most productive medium for the advertiser whose product appeals to a limited group.

Advertising Rates

The following figures, which represent recent rates, show how the advertising space in magazines is valued. Do the returns from the advertising warrant such large expenditures? The fact that the same business firms use space year after year, and in some cases pay an advance in order to obtain a preferred position that is much in demand, indicates the profitable experience of big buyers of advertising space.

Advertising Costs for Selected Magazines

Magazine	Average Monthly Circulation	Cost for Full Page B/.W Ad	Cost Per 1,000 Readers For B/W Ad	Cost for Full Page 4-Color Ad	Cost Per 1,000 Readers 4-Color Ad
ESQUIRE	650,083	$ 8,950	$13.77	$13,400	$20.62
FIELD & STREAM	2,000,000	16,600	8.30	24.960	12.48
GOOD HOUSEKEEPING	5,000,000	36,045	7.21	45.235	9.05
MC CALL'S	6,199,690	40,050	6.46	49,250	7.94
NEWSWEEK	2,950,000	33,160	11.24	51,730	17.54
READER'S DIGEST	17,766,230	68,400	3.85	82,200	4.63

THEATER PROGRAMS

Theater programs can be an important medium of advertising. Over 150,000 programs are distributed each week in New York City alone, and proportionate quantities are distributed in other large cities. Most of the theater programs in these large cities are prepared by specialists who make advertising their business and construct the programs in order to

Circulation and markets for the popular *Playbill* theater program.

PLAYBILL
Average Monthly Circulation

		%
New York-Metropolitan Area	718,080	70.4
Out-of-Town (excluding N.Y.-Met. Area)	301,920	29.6
	1,020,000	100.0

Major Market Breakdown

New York-Metropolitan Area	718,080	

Top Ten Markets (excluding N.Y.-Met. Area)
(Rank order by circulation)

1. Philadelphia	26,572		
2. Baltimore/Washington, D.C.	18,419		
3. Chicago	13,286		
4. Boston	11,174		
5. Los Angeles	9,965		
6. Detroit	8,457		
7. San Francisco	6,040		
8. Dallas/Ft. Worth	4,229		
9. Atlanta	3,021		
10. St. Louis	3,021		
Total Top Ten Markets	104,184	104,184	
Other Markets	197,736	197,736	
	301,920	1,020,000	

give them maximum advertising value. Interesting material concerning the play and the players is so arranged as to lead the playgoer to read the advertising before the curtain rises and between acts. Since such programs are frequently preserved, their advertising value is increased.

The fact that a person attends a theater is an indication that he may have money to spend for luxuries. The theater program, therefore, is a medium for advertising luxuries rather than staple merchandise. Hotels, restaurants, jewelry, furs, liquors, airlines, banks, and perfumes are frequently advertised, although there is no reason why local merchants cannot be represented as well.

A favorable factor in program advertising is that the advertisement reaches the reader at a time when he is carefree and, hence, in a mood to receive favorable impressions. Audiences of the great metropolitan theaters contain many transients and suburban residents. Visitors to the city frequently combine shopping trips with visits to the theater. People living at a distance sometimes plan two or three such trips a year. The advertiser should remember these facts in purchasing space and in preparing his copy.

Interested advertisers should contact *Playbill* sales in New York City and other urban areas for advertising rates and other pertinent information.

MASS ADVERTISING

For exposure to wider and more general audiences, mass advertising in the form of outdoor signs, directories, and window displays can be effective.

Outdoor Advertising

Over the last few years, there have been rapid developments in the artistic qualities and the effectiveness of outdoor advertising. The painted sign, the poster, and the electric sign have all taken on new, attractive elements. The Outdoor Advertising Association of America has standardized methods of doing advertising business and has thus made possible uniform service all over the country. The large plant operators have constructed attractive billboards of uniform design from Maine to California. The plant operator leases space to an advertiser, then puts the advertisement on the board, and keeps it in condition according to the terms of the contract.

Examples of outdoor advertising.

Furthermore, to meet the needs of advertisers who wish to do poster advertising on a national scale, Outdoor Advertising, Inc. has representatives in many American cities. This agency represents plant operators in various parts of the country, and it arranges contracts for poster display anywhere in the country.

The last few years have seen great strides in the use of electricity in advertising. The neon sign has turned the advertising night into day, making Broadway in New York City the greatest advertising medium in the world.

Electric spectaculars have made possible wonderful color effects and, through the mechanical control of switches, they produce the effect of motion, which is an important element in attracting attention. Words spelled out letter by letter, and even sentences produced word by word, appeal to the instinct of curiosity and, as such, are strong in attention value. By the same principle, a product may be shown in operation or in

28

The electric sign is an attention-getter.

Additional examples of outdoor advertising.

use, thereby not only attracting attention by its motion, but also creating interest through the message it carries. It must be remembered that this form of advertising is very expensive in both its construction and its operation.

Outdoor advertising is sometimes used as a primary medium, but more often it is used to supplement other forms of advertising. Such a wide variety of products have been advertised with apparent success by this supplementary form that it is difficult to state for what kinds of products outdoor advertising is best adapted. It would seem logical that only products of mass consumption or products naturally purchased by a large percentage of the viewers should be advertised through this medium, but we find high-priced automobiles, investments, real estate, and printing continually advertised on billboards. The producers of food products, laundry articles, cosmetics, beverages, devices for amusement, and wearing apparel have successfully used this medium to promote sales.

The copy treatment must be very different from that of other forms of advertising. The advertiser must remember that his audience is always in motion, sometimes pleasure-bent, and is in no mood for argument. The form of appeal must be bold, simple, expressive, and suggestive. No more than a quick passing glance can be counted on, and the message must be flashed to a mind that is keyed to grasp the import of changing and moving objects. Details must be eliminated, and only one or two ideas can be given great prominence. The most successful copy usually has few words, often not more than five, and tells a complete story by means of a picture.

The use of color in outdoor advertising makes it possible to produce panels of great attention and interest value and, at the same time, of artistic merit. Package goods can be shown in their true colors, food products can be given realistic and tempting representation, and clothing can be stylishly displayed.

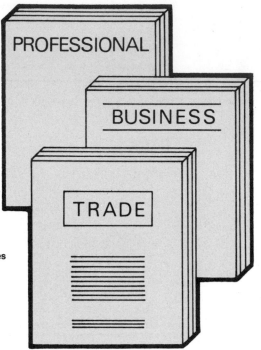

Directories provide lists of available products and services in a given field.

Directory Advertising

Numerous directories are published throughout the United States and many of them carry a large amount of advertising — *Who's Who, The Blue Book of the Shoe and Leather Industry, Wool Trade Directory*, and countless others.

All directories serve one purpose: to provide people with sources that offer products or services they need. As such, they provide a ready-made market.

The listings are organized for easy access — by advertiser name, when included under a general heading, or by product or service.

The most widely used are the *Yellow Pages* telephone directory. In this directory you are entitled to one free listing as a telephone subscriber. Beyond this, if you wish to emphasize your name in bold type or use more space for a display ad, you are charged for it.

Also, if you are a dealer or distributor of a brand-name product, the manufacturer usually pays for the trade-name space and you may be listed without charge.

Practically every trade or profession has a directory of its own that lists its members. This is a useful and often free medium of advertising.

There are general industrial directories that list products useful to other industries, and these are grouped under a common heading such as wool, metal, etc. Other directories cover all industries, with thousands of classifications.

A section from the often used *Yellow Pages.*

These directories may be found in the *Yellow Pages* under Publishers of Trade and Business Publications.

For the smaller merchant, the *Yellow Pages* can offer the best and most useful medium. Your local telephone company business office will discuss your needs with you if you call and ask to speak to a representative.

Window Displays

It has been determined that, in a city of 100,000 inhabitants, about 18,000 people pass a well-located window each day. The value of a store window depends upon the location of the store; the importance of the location being determined, in turn, by the number of people passing. In fact, the value of a store window for display purposes has a great influence on the rent charged. The proprietors of many large retail stores realize the value of their windows for advertising purposes and therefore consider window use as a major operating expense for their different departments' rent in the same way that they distribute overhead costs for lighting or newspaper space. Many retailers consider windows to be as much as one-quarter of their advertising expense. At the same time they expect their window advertising to produce from 30 to 40 percent of their sales.

Manufacturers realize how important store advertising is for their products, and, therefore, include the obtaining of retail store window space in their merchandising plans. Knowing that small retailers often give little attention to their window displays, the manufacturer sometimes sends out well-trained salesmen to help small retailers make attractive window displays with his product. Many manufacturers' first efforts in providing dealer aids have been in window displays. They may provide background dummies, photographs, and ideas so that dealers can make their own displays. In this way the dealer gets the benefit of expert advice, while both the manufacturer and the dealer gain from increased sales.

Following are some of the most useful methods for creating effective window displays.

1. The display should be unified and contain only one thing or a group of very closely related things. However, if several unrelated things need to be shown, low partitions may be used to divide the space into smaller sections so that there will be unity in each section.

2. The background should be simple so as not to draw attention away from the merchandise displayed. It should also harmonize in color with the merchandise. Mirrors are often used to give the effect of a larger window and also to show rear views when clothing is displayed.

3. Proper balance and proportions should be maintained. This principle usually means placing shorter articles to the front and taller articles at the rear. No amount of direction, however, can produce the proper effect since none but the artistic eye can determine what is best.

4. There should be a center of interest, and everything displayed should direct attention toward that point. When a window is heaped full of merchandise, attention cannot be focused on any single thing.

Even though these two window displays are quite dissimilar, they both have achieved unity and balance through the use of simple backgrounds, proportional displays, and multiple lighting.

32

5. Real or suggested animation, movement, or the representation of a product in use offers power of attraction. Just as animation gives life and interest to a picture, so action adds attractiveness to a window display.

6. A display that has a timely interest is likely to receive much more attention than one that does not. It is unwise, however, to sacrifice interest for the sake of attention. Displays of animals and other things foreign to the merchandise sold in the store may attract attention, but as a rule will not gain interest, and will not result in sales.

7. The display must be constructed so that its full significance is grasped by a short glance. The time that a passerby spends stopped at a window averages less than fifteen seconds, and the majority of passersby do not stop at all.

8. The display must be changed frequently. A display usually outlives its usefulness in about five days.

9. Lighting is a very important part of window advertising. The light must be softened so that it will not blind the observer. It must also emanate from several points so that unpleasant shadows will not be cast. The variety of available lighting fixtures and colors of electric bulbs make it possible to produce very attractive and effective windows.

It must be remembered, however, that the test of a good window display is not "Is it beautiful?" but "Does it center attention on the merchandise?" and "Does it sell the goods?"

DIRECT ADVERTISING

Sizes and lengths of mailing lists vary greatly.

Direct advertising includes those forms of advertising that are addressed to prospective buyers individually. It differs from the other forms of advertising, which appeal to consumers in groups. The billboard, for example, is placed where "he who runs may read"; but, in direct advertising, specific material is placed in the hands of designated individuals. The material for such advertising includes catalogs, enclosures, letters, samples, handbills, novelties, announcements, blotters, calendars, house organs, booklets, package inserts, price lists, and many other kinds of advertising matter. It may be presented by the salesman, a special messenger, or the mailman. Direct-mail advertising is direct advertising through the mails.

Uses of Direct Advertising

Direct advertising has aptly been explained as follows: as a pathfinder, as an introduction, as a salesman, as a reminder, as a goodwill builder, as a means of increasing sales, as an elixir for active customers, as a tonic for sick customers, and as a pulmonator for practically dead customers.

Direct advertising is also used advantageously in missionary work preceding the visit of the salesman and in sorting out interested prospects on a mailing list. A folder containing vigorous sales appeals may be mailed with an attached reply card to those on the list. This may be followed up by mail with more direct sales matter or by the visit of a salesman.

Four-page folder (broadside) with sealer and space for address opens to 16" x 21" (41 x 53 cm) and is ready for mailing.

Booklet cover is 5¾" x 5¾" (15 x 15 cm).

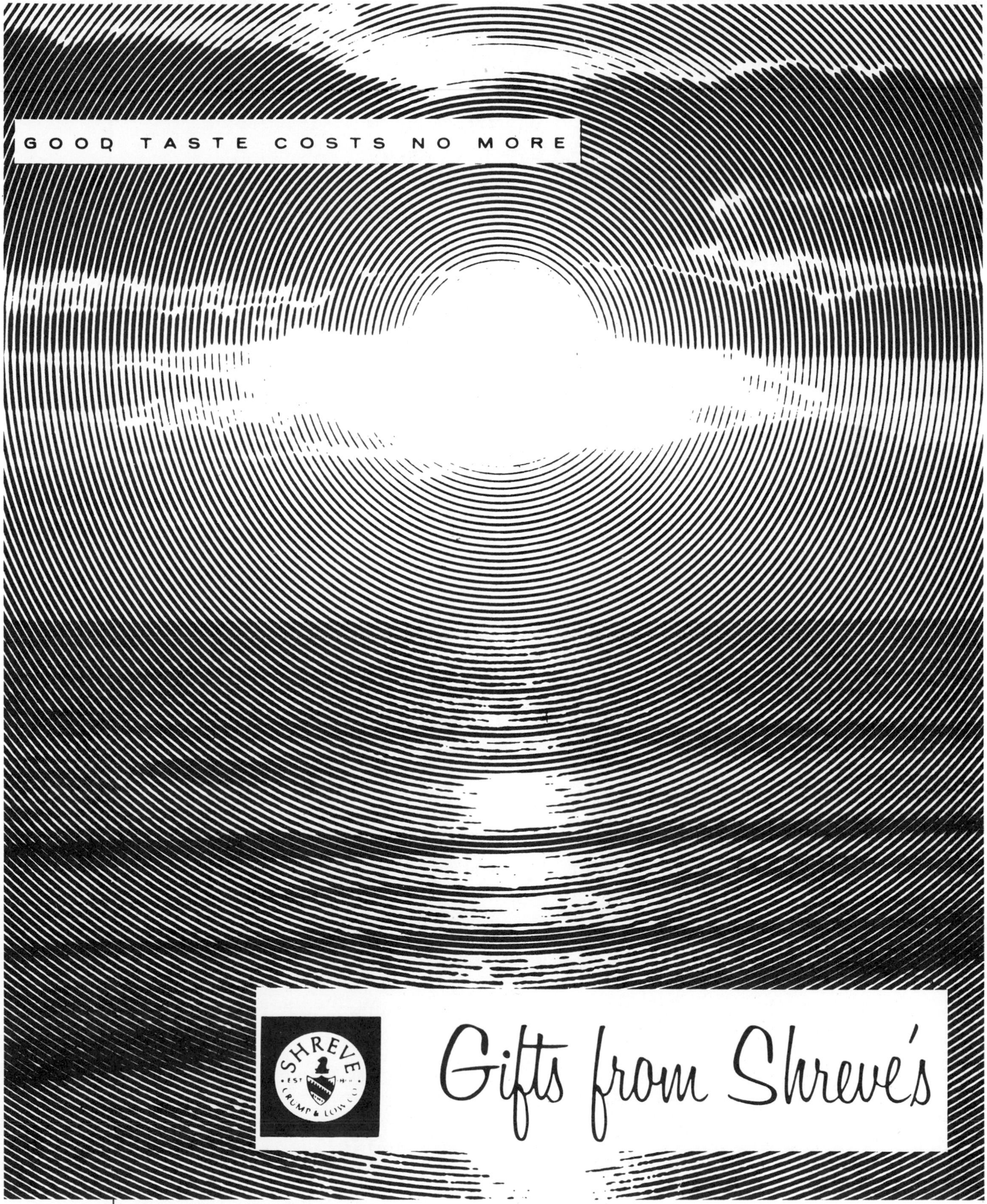
GOOD TASTE COSTS NO MORE
SHREVE
EST
CRUMP & LOW CO
Gifts from Shreve's

Multipage catalog measures 8¼″ x 10″
(21 x 25 cm).

Cover of twelve-page calendar, 8" x 8" (20 x 20 cm), with discount coupon on each page.

BURGER KING BICENTENNIAL
1976 BICENTENNIAL COUPON CALENDAR
BICENTENNIAL COUPON CALENDAR
BICENTENNIAL COUPON CALENDAR
BICENTENNIAL COUPON CALENDAR
BICENTENNIAL COUPON CALENDAR
BICENTENNIAL COUPON CALENDAR

...CAL EVENTS IN THE BIRTH OF THE U.S. • COLORFUL AND FACT-FILLED.

Supplemental Health Insurance Program for Retired Teachers

Retired Teachers Chapter
of the
United Federation of Teachers

260 Park Avenue South
New York, N.Y. 10010

For a full discussion of the program attend the membership meeting.

**Nov. 9   1:00 P.M.
Marc Ballroom
Union Square**

Twelve-page information booklet is 3¾" x 8¾" (10 x 22 cm).

Twelve-page calendar, 7¾" x 8¾" (20 x 22 cm), with sales message on each page.

January 1976

Benjamin Franklin—born January 17, 1706—printer, inventor, scientist, writer, philosopher and framer of the Declaration of Independence.

FEBRUARY
S M T W T F S
1 2 3 4 5 6 7
8 9 10 11 12 13 14
15 16 17 18 19 20 21
22 23 24 25 26 27 28
29

Sun	Mon	Tues	Wed	Thur	Fri	Sat
				1 New Year's Day 1863-Emancipation Proclamation signed	2	3 1942-Japanese capture Manila
4	5 1943-George Washington Carver dies	6 1941-Franklin D. Roosevelt's "Four Freedoms" speech	7	8	9	10 1776-Tom Paine publishes "Common Sense", demanding independence
11 1785-Capitol moved to New York City	12	13	14	15 1929-Birthdate of Martin Luther King, Jr.	16	17 1706-Birthdate of Benjamin Franklin
18	19	20	21 1816-African Methodist Episcopal Church founded	22	23 1973-Peace treaty signed with North Vietnam	24
25	26	27	28	29	30	31

Buy one Double Meat Hamburger and get another Double Meat Hamburger FREE.*
See reverse side for details.
Good at any participating Burger King restaurant.

Direct advertising lends itself to emphasis of special sales and to concentration on special articles or groups of articles. Because circulation is under the complete control of the advertiser, the advertising material may be personal and select, or impersonal and general — whatever seems necessary. If the advertising is issued repeatedly, the product or service may achieve the status of a "household word." Also, any major change in advertising form or content will be more noticeable if the advertising has been previously issued on many occasions.

For a ...

living room

dining room

bedroom...

you can live in!

This small catalog or booklet measures
4¼" x 5½" (11 x 14 cm).

Dear Neighbor,

You are invited to help us demonstrate that our gifts are as much fun to choose as they are to receive.

So we are enclosing a booklet to give you a few ideas before your visit.

We have selected an enchanting array of giftware. Our buyers have traveled the continents to bring you this unique collection.

We know you will enjoy your visit, and fall in love with our gift-giving ideas.

Sincerely,

Philip Herman

Philip Herman, President

Circular letter with booklet enclosure is
5¼" x 5¼" (13 x 13 cm).

Advantages of Direct-Mail Advertising

Direct-mail advertising has certain unique advantages; the primary advantage being that its distribution can be regulated and confined to a certain group of people in a well-defined territory, e.g., the advertising material may be addressed to doctors, lawyers, or farmers in a specified locale.

Direct-mail advertising enables the advertiser to develop the process of selective selling to the maximum degree of efficiency. Its proper use is definitely with those groups or classes of people who can be reached more economically and more certainly through the mails than through mediums of general circulation. Newspaper advertising makes it possible to break down the national market into sectional or local markets and to concentrate sales activity in certain cities or sections of the country in which business is good. Direct-mail advertising makes it possible to break down local markets into various classifications involving practically every form of human activity and every degree of social, political, or financial standing, and to reach those within these classifications by means of an individual rather than a mass appeal.

Another advantage is its unimpeded access to the consumer: no one ever coldly dismisses the letter carrier by parting the window curtains and motioning for him to go away (while canvassers and salesmen have to struggle to get the door open the smallest crack).

The Direct-Mail Marketing Association, Inc. gives the following advantages of direct advertising:

1. Your messages are direct and personal, being placed in the hands of the persons to whom they are addressed or to whom they are given.

2. Your messages need not shout for attention. They are alone with the reader.

3. Your messages can be timed to reach your customers, present or prospective, on the day or the month or the season when they should be received for maximum results.

4. You can single out your prospects and extend your personality beyond the limits of impersonal contact to create confidence in you and the product or service you are selling.

5. There is no waste circulation. You pay only for the directing of your messages to those you want to reach, thus, direct advertising is economical.

6. Your messages, through the copy, will be read because you are talking to your customers or prospects in the language they understand.

7. You can tell as complete a story as is needed with as accurate and fine illustrations as may be called for.

8. Finally, direct advertising is a selling force that will produce immediate action and is cumulative in its pulling power.

Circular Duplicating Letters

Machines (photocopying equipment, printing presses) for the reproduction of letters make the circular letter an inexpensive and effective means of advertising for some kinds of businesses. This duplicated letter, however, in comparison with the typewritten letter, gets little attention. If the personal element is an important factor in the advertising, it may pay to have duplicate copies individually prepared. This can be relatively inexpensive if modern word processing equipment, such as magnetic tape typewriters, are used. This equipment may be purchased, leased, or rented for continuous use by the do-it-yourself type, or a local printer may provide this service on a per-job basis.

Of course, letters that appear to be prepared individually carry more weight than mass-produced circular letters. But the letter will be successful provided it carries a message of such interest, or is so attractive in form, that it will be read. The test, of course, is whether or not the letter is read.

The best rule for the advertiser to follow in preparing a circular letter is to study carefully other circular letters that have been successful.

The most important part of a circular or a follow-up letter is the first line. Such advertising matter that is commonplace, ordinary, or hackneyed goes into the wastepaper basket unread. Originality, leavened with good taste, is the first requisite in preparing the advertising material. To this must be added the advertiser's ability to visualize a particular customer as a type and to direct the message to this individual in as personal a way as possible. With a circular letter it may be possible to use an enclosure, such as a pamphlet, a folder, a stuffer, or any other advertising form. The enclosure should be mentioned in the letter.

Catalogs

A catalog may be defined as a list of articles with prices and descriptions or explanations. It contains useful information for a prospective customer and is, therefore, generally kept for reference. Large mail-order houses issue periodic catalogs containing descriptions and prices of almost all articles used by human beings. Their general catalog sometimes contains more than one thousand pages. They often issue special catalogs covering selected groups of articles. Large catalogs may be in loose-leaf form so that, as changes are made, the old pages (or leaves) can be taken out and new ones inserted.

Alternate cover designs for automotive parts catalogs.

The catalog in general has become very impressive in its composition. Since it is often the sole guide some customers use in making purchases, its clarity, courtesy, and brevity are relied upon for sales. The articles are described in language so full of selling force that it is almost impossible to resist buying.

Color illustrations have proven profitable and have made catalogs more attractive. Everything possible is done to make the commodity look as real as possible. One mail-order house that does a yearly business of more than $100 million has built up this vast volume of business through their heavily illustrated catalogs. The picture is in most cases a faithful representation of the article. It has been estimated that a catalog with color illustrations that represent the articles realistically has fifteen times more drawing power than a catalog printed in black-and-white. The commodities in a catalog should be arranged by group so that they can be found easily in the table of contents or the index.

Booklets

A booklet is used to present the selling points of a commodity. Its purpose is to make the particular commodity it describes attractive and desirable. All factors such as style of type, balance and harmony in makeup, illustrations, border display, and quality paper are essential. A booklet may be bound attractively and illustrated artistically. The general impression created by it must reflect the nature of the article sold and the image of the advertiser. A booklet is prepared in the same way as other advertising copy, that is, by means of a series of layouts. The final layout is called the dummy.

A possible cover for a bartender's booklet on tequila recipes.

A booklet usually goes into detail concerning the commodity advertised. It may explain the production of the materials as, for example, in the silk industry. It may set forth the superiority of the article by describing special features, the manufacturing process, and the economy, wear, or comfort of the article.

A booklet usually confines itself to one article or one set of articles, and may vary from a few pages to one hundred or more. It may present, in addition, a summarized statement of the firm's other products.

Broadsides

A broadside is usually a form of direct advertising that attempts to produce results through the use of large display. Very often it is the size of a newspaper page, is folded and held together by a seal, and has a place for the mailing address. It is often used in advertising to dealers because one side may be used to present the selling points for the dealer's information, while the other side may be used by the dealer as poster display.

A folded broadside using a large display.

A folder can provide direct-mail economy.

Folders

A folder is somewhat smaller than a broadside and is folded. Since no hard-and-fast rule governs its use, the folder has almost limitless possibilities. Furthermore, it is probably the most economical piece of direct-advertising literature. Many clever and novel attention-getting devices can be used, and the artistic possibilities are unlimited.

Package Inserts

Package inserts, an inexpensive ad packaged with a product, may perform several functions.

1. They may advertise other products of the same manufacturer. The insert may be in the form of a descriptive coupon that invites the user to send for a sample.

2. Package inserts may be used to ensure the proper use of goods. The successful use of food products often depends on adequate directions; textile products often require special care in cleansing; mechanical products must be installed and adjusted according to directions. Additional uses of the goods may be suggested by a package insert, and in that way, the demand may be increased.

Package inserts are appropriate for additional advertising after an initial sale.

Novelty Advertising

The calendar is probably the most widely used article in novelty advertising. Pencils, rulers, thermometers, paperweights, and many other articles are also used. Firms specializing in these items are listed in most *Yellow Pages*.

House Organs

About thirty-five hundred house organs are issued regularly in the United States. Most of them are in the form of small magazines that are issued monthly or biweekly. Two distinct types of house organs are published by manufacturers or distributors for the purpose of stimulating sales. The first type is planned primarily for the benefit of employees, salesmen, branch houses, or distributors. These publications give news items concerning personal and social events, suggestions to salesmen or dealers, information concerning new merchandise, and policies and methods of the concern. Their object is to stimulate business by welding the entire organization together with a sound business spirit and enthusiasm.

The second type of house organ is planned primarily for prospects and consumers. Publications of this type are really service bulletins that give information concerning coming events of the business, style changes, and the presentation of the product in a subtle way. In both types of house organs the aim is to increase direct and personal relations with customers by acquainting them with the ideals, policies, and purposes of the company and to create a better knowledge of the merchandise carried in stock.

Mailing Lists

Perhaps the most important factor in direct-mail advertising is the mailing list. Julius Rosenwald of Sears-Roebuck once said:

"If some unthinkable catastrophe should come about tonight and wipe away all Sears-Roebuck buildings and merchandise, I should not worry especially, as long as our mailing list escaped. We could erect new buildings, buy new merchandise, and carry on at once; but if the names of our customers were lost, we should have to begin again from the very beginning."

The basic idea behind mailing lists is to have only those individuals who might be interested in a particular product or service receive the mail concerning it.

There are many different ways people get on mailing lists intended to serve their special interests: they subscribe, join, purchase, or charge. They request catalogs and buy from them, clip and respond to coupons, and declare their interests on magazine reader service cards.

Mailing lists are generally costly and difficult to develop and maintain. Careful maintenance is essential if lists are to be truly accurate and selective, containing only addresses of individuals likely to have a genuine interest in a given topic. The rate of return to an advertiser from a carefully compiled list is sufficiently attractive that direct marketers are willing to pay a substantial premium for the use of such lists.

For these reasons, mailing lists are not sold but rented, or exchanged. Moreover, they are rented for one time use only. Generally, lists are rented in the form of a single set of labels or a magnetic tape for use on a computer. Occasionally, the advertiser provides envelopes for addressing.

Mailing lists may be rented directly from the companies or organizations that develop the lists or from brokers. Like other brokers, a mailing-list broker acts as an agent between owner and client. The list broker maintains records of mailing lists available for rental from various sources and of their rental prices (usually quoted as so much per one-thousand names). The list user (advertiser) rents lists for one-time use and pays no charge to the broker for this service. The broker is paid by the list owner on a percentage basis. Usually, reputable brokers have access to all available mailing lists. And usually, five thousand, which is considered a test quantity, is the minimum number of names rented. These brokers are listed in directories or through The Direct Mail/Marketing Association, with members in forty-eight states.

Some of the classifications for available lists are:

Stockholders of national corporations

Home owners

Men and women in specified cities, classified by income

Men and women classified by occupation or age

Automobile owners classified by make of car

TRANSIT ADVERTISING

Most people think of transit (subways, elevators, commuter trains, and buses) as a means of getting to and from work — and it is. But, surprisingly, more people ride transit for shopping than for employment. Among women, 56 percent ride transit for shopping. This figure is particularly significant: it means transit can be the last advertising impression a shopper gets before she actually makes a purchase.

The transit medium is a good vehicle for advertising that seeks action. It is seen by consumers in local markets close to retail outlets. Transit advertising affords both national and local advertisers low-cost penetration and coverage of selected markets. It provides frequency and continuity of ad impressions to repeat audiences of working riders. It extends advertising exposure potential by its continued presence and visibility to mass transit users. The medium is used by national and local advertisers for both broad and selective market coverage. Exterior bus displays, interior advertisements, station posters, and other displays in selected locations make possible massive product and brand exposure in striking color. These can be placed at or near buying locations that expose a sales message repeatedly during a particular showing. Transit advertisements reach varied audiences: both men and women traveling to and from employment, housewives during the daytime shopping hours, college students, and children.

For the local advertiser, transit's flexibility permits advertisements to be tailored to specific markets and to reach riders along transit routes passing particular retail outlets. Transit also provides retailers low-cost and possibly multiple exposure close to point of sale. It is used by department stores, financial institutions, newspapers, magazines, radio, and television stations for editorial and program promotion (indicating that competing media are aware of transit's value), and by many other local advertisers. For both local and national advertisers, transit advertisements can be most attractive in format, impression value, makeup, and content.

This is a striking subway platform poster.

Products can be displayed to full advantage in one or more colors or in black-and-white. The medium offers creative latitude in format, illustration, and color to add interest and originality for prospect-winning attention.

The Transit Environment

Transit advertising is part of the environment in which the consumer lives and travels. Transit riders are mobile people who live in the heart of major markets and usually spend more waking time away from home than at home. College students in urban centers are an example. A large percentage commute from school to home during and after semesters. The worth of the college market has been placed at $21 billion, exclusive of tuition, room, and board. Because of lower living expenses, college students actually spend 37 percent more for some consumer goods than the average American. For example, the average college female spends $650 per year for her clothing compared to about $250 spent by the average woman.

Advantages of Transit Advertising

Among the numerous advantages of transit advertising are the following:

1. This form of advertising can be localized to a particular transit line of a city, or a section of the country, or it can be made national.

2. Transit advertising can hold the attention of passengers at a time when there is little else to occupy their minds.

3. The average passenger spends from ten to twenty-five minutes on a bus or subway. If the advertisement makes an initial impression on the reader, there is time to get the whole story.

4. The artistic possibilities are unlimited.

5. A transit advertisement may be the last reminder to the shopper before the store is entered.

6. The general tone of the advertisement is kept high through the supervision of the advertising company controlling the space.

7. All classes of people and practically the entire population of some cities ride quite frequently.

8. The rate per 1,000 exposures for this medium is probably lower than that for any other.

The Cost of Transit Advertising

One of the biggest selling points of transit advertising is that it provides advertising impressions at extremely low cost. On a national average, the cost per 1,000 exposures for inside transit advertising is between fifteen and twenty cents. For outside bus posters, it averages less than seven cents per 1,000. You can make your own comparison with other local media and readily see how far the advertising budget goes if spent on transit advertising.

The Transit Medium

Transit advertising comprises two distinct mediums: interior displays reaching commuters, travelers, and shoppers; and exterior vehicle displays reaching residents, visitors, businessmen, and motorists on transit routes. Inside transit offers frequency, continuity, and repetition of advertising impact. It reaches more than one-third of its monthly riders on any single day. A transit rider averages twenty-four rides per month, sixty-one minutes a day. In comparing the income classifications of the national population with transit rider income, the latter closely parallels the entire national distribution.

The car card is an inside transit advertising display. Most common size is 11" x 28" (28 x 71 cm) and runs up to 11" x 56" (28 x 142 cm).

Traveling display, 21" x 44" (53 x 112 cm), is an outside transit advertising display that is usually shown on the sides and sometimes on the front of vehicles.

Advertising spaces are available on sides of local buses.

TRAVELING DISPLAY

QUEEN SIZE

Exterior displays travel on buses through and to urban and suburban business areas and shopping centers. Bus mobility takes exterior displays to many locations in the same day. They provide continuous, multiple advertisement exposures to a variety of audiences. Transit advertising, whether interior or exterior, is always close to shoppers and prospects at or near retail outlets.

Transit Advertising Space

Transit advertising is carried by more than 70,000 vehicles (buses, subways, rapid transit, and commuter trains) in markets nationally. The transit advertising medium meets the requirements of measurement, standardization, and certified circulation for nationwide advertising media as described in the Standard Rate and Date Service.

Front-end or headlight display is an outside display placed on the front of vehicles. Common sizes are 21″ x 44″ (53 x 112 cm) and 11″ x 42″ (28 x 107 cm).

Queen-size poster 30″ x 88″ (76 x 223 cm) is an outside display placed on the sides of vehicles (usually the curb side).

King-size poster, 30″ x 144″ (76 x 366 cm), is an outside transit display placed on the sides of vehicles.

Rear-end display measures 21″ x 72″ (53 x 183 cm).

Transit Advertising:

Interior. Interior displays may be printed in any number of colors, using silk screen or lithography for printing. Sizes (height by width) are available in 11″ x 21″ (28 x 53 cm), 22″ x 21″ (56 x 53 cm), 11″ x 28″ (28 x 71 cm), 11″ x 56″ (28 x 142 cm), 16″ x 44″ (41 x 112 cm). They provide the advertiser with a wide variety of size and display options to suit advertising objectives.

"Take Ones," available in postcard stock pads, may be attached to interior advertising displays where direct consumer response to advertisements is desired.

Exterior. Busoramas are rooftop illuminated transit advertising panels backlighted by means of fluorescent tubes. They are displayed on buses by laminating a vinyl sheet containing the advertiser's copy to the per-

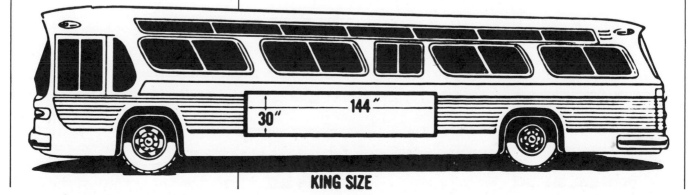

KING SIZE

Busorama is the trade name for back-lighted advertising displays that appear on rooftops of vehicle exteriors. The overall panel size is 21⅛" x 144¾" (55 x 368 cm).

manent face of the display area. King Size Displays, 30" x 144" (76 x 366 cm), are exterior posters appearing on the sides of buses. Advertising copy can be silk screened onto composition board, or silk screened or lithographed onto paper (provided by the advertiser) that is pasted onto hardboard. Queen Size Displays, 30" x 88" (76 x 224 cm), are exterior positions appearing on the sides of buses. Reproduction methods are similar to those for King Size Displays. Traveling Displays are standard exterior advertising displays. Positions of the displays vary with the market. Taillight Spectaculars, 21" x 72" (53 x 183 cm), are exterior transit ads appearing on the rear of buses.

One-sheet 46" x 30" (117 x 76 cm) is a poster displayed on station platforms.

Two-sheet 46" x 60" (117 x 152 cm) is a poster displayed on station platforms.

Station Posters

Major urban centers including New York, Chicago, Philadelphia, Washington, D.C., and Boston have subway or elevated lines. Station posters, therefore, provide a medium for national and local advertising in these cities. These posters are of the following uniform sizes: 1-sheet, 30" x 46" (76 x 117 cm); 2-sheet, 46" x 60" (117 x 152 cm); 3-sheet, 42" x 84" (107 x 213 cm). The posters are placed opposite platforms, where they are in full view of waiting passengers. This advertising is controlled by the same companies that control car-card advertising, and contracts can be arranged through them in the same way. Special transit displays such as illuminated clocks, lighted, colorful signs with three-dimensional optical effects, and a variety of other visually compelling display designs are available at select locations in train, subway, and bus terminals as well as at station platforms and other heavy consumer traffic locations.

Buying Transit Advertising

Advertisers can schedule transit advertisements in an individual market or in any combination of 380 American markets. Rates are quoted for showings on a monthly basis. Inside displays are bought on full, half, or quarter showings — all, half, or a quarter of the vehicles in a fleet. Outside

Here is an example of "Take Ones."

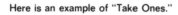

Square end 22" x 21" (56 x 53 cm) is an inside display located near doors and is considered premium space in rail vehicles.

displays are sold on a unit basis. Market characteristics vary. Transit advertising companies provide a range of display and size choices for exterior showings in a market. Discounts are usually granted for three-month, six-month, or twelve-month contracts.

Transit Merchandising

Take Ones, referred to in the Transit Advertising Space section, give the advertiser a means of securing action at the point of advertising impact.

47

Clock spectacular is a backlighted display accompanying a large clock. A moving message may also be part of the display.

These order or inquiry forms are attached to the transit advertisement and may be removed singly by prospects responding to the advertising offer. They make direct and immediate response to the advertising message possible.

Size and Position

Transit advertising offers a wide range of sizes and positions. Advertisements within the transit vehicle can be placed along each side and in special positions. Outside display units are available on the side, front, and rear of vehicles. King sizes may be secured on either or both sides of a bus. Other sizes are available on front and rear locations. Two-sheet, three-sheet, and six-sheet station posters provide various sizes and strategic platform locations for attention-getting advertising messages. These and other availabilities permit an advertiser great flexibility in selecting locations and sizes to meet both budgetary and advertising campaign objectives.

For information concerning rates, etc., contact the local bus company for referral to the firm handling bus advertising, or contract: Nation-wide Bus Advertising Company, 423 Park Avenue South, New York, New York 10016.

Top-end or over-door is an inside transit display measuring 16″ x 39″ (41 x 99 cm) and 16″ x 44″ (41 x 112 cm). It is considered premium space in rail vehicles and is usually located over intervehicle doors.

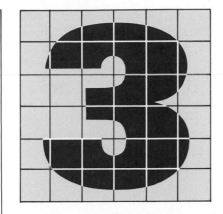

THE COPY

How to write an ad that will convert readers into buyers

Get More satisfaction.

THE COPY

By "copy" we refer to the message in your ad that usually consists of a heading and follow-up text. If you are concerned with the selling of products or services, the importance of the copy in an ad cannot be overstated.

Beautiful pictures may evoke the admiration of the public, startling headlines may capture the attention of millions, humorous jingles may become more familiar than the national anthem, but unless readers are turned into buyers, the advertising has failed its purpose. This purpose is rarely achieved without sufficient attention to copy.

GENERAL DIRECTIONS FOR WRITING COPY

Clarity and force are characteristics of effective copy. These qualities are usually best achieved when the copy is grammatically correct. Slight liberties occasionally make the copy more interesting, but careless deviation from accepted usage is not to be condoned. However, it is more important that the reader gets the right idea concerning the product than that the grammar be faultless.

The advertisement should bubble with enthusiasm. This does not mean that exaggeration or meaningless superlatives are necessary. Note the enthusiasm conveyed by the following: "*Meet spring halfway with a big bowl of Kellogg's Corn Flakes for breakfast. They're full of refreshment. Rich in energy and easy to digest.*" Vigor and animation make this copy alive and challenge the interest of the reader.

Here are some examples of provocative copy that can easily be converted to use for other products and services.

The free lunch was never free.

How to take someone out for a holiday dinner when you can't be there.

"You can prospect for out-of-town accounts without leaving town, and we'll scramble to show you how."

Four of the 400 things you can do without flash.

Vague superlatives should always be omitted in favor of concrete description. "*The Best Hats in Town*," "*The Highest Grade of Materials*," and "*The Greatest Bargains*" are meaningless phrases.

Personification or the presentation of an advertised product by the human form is very often helpful in impressing that product on the mind of the public. Such figures as Mr. Clean, Charley the Tuna, the Jolly Green Giant, and the Pillsbury Dough Boy are as well known as characters from Dickens. Care must be exercised not to overemphasize the personification in such a way as to divert attention from the product.

Principles of Good Copy

The copywriter should also observe the following principles: be brief and to the point. Write in the present tense as much as possible. Use verbs of action. In place of the pronouns I, we, ours, my, and mine, use you, your, and yours. Assume the consumer's viewpoint and remember that of the three — the manufacturer, the article, and the consumer — the consumer is most important. With an open mind you may be amazed at what you will learn. Be a model for clean-cut expression. Inspire with honest statements. Learn to select just the words that will drive home the sales message with the least amount of mental effort from a reader. Cultivate an affirmative attitude. Finally, test the advertisement for clarity by submitting it to friends for interpretation.

The only thing more impressive than our name is your name.

Say "Merry Christmas!" all year long.

the best surprise is no surprise.

These are additional examples of stimulating headlines.

Quick! Send for "Nasty Jack" before you mix your next drink.

Before you spend $8,000 or more for a motor home, spend $1.95 for this.

When it comes to buying a color TV, the last thing to trust is your luck.

Importance of Words

When we consider the vast amount of money expended for advertising and the startling influence that advertising has upon the life of every human being in this country, we can appreciate that clarity, conciseness, and force are great considerations in writing advertisements. Words, sentences, paragraphs, whole compositions — even punctuation marks — have concrete value in real dollars and cents. Any blunder in the selection of words in advertising may result in severe financial loss.

The importance of the few words that make up the headline cannot be overestimated. They capture the reader's attention and stimulate his further interest in the advertisement. Since the gist of the appeal is usually contained in those four or five words, the effectiveness of the entire advertisement often depends on how successfully these words are chosen.

Next to the headline, the most vital part of the advertisement is the copy, or text. The copywriter must know (1) what the advertiser's product or service is and (2) how best to expose that product to the public. His medium — words — must express and impress.

Any successful advertisement probably has made use of these principles: unity, coherence, and emphasis. Unity means that the advertisement has one outstanding point which is adhered to. Unity demands that neither too much material nor too many ideas are put in one advertisement. An advertisement should not be made a carryall. The appeals or selling points should be selected and presented *one at a time*. They may be presented separately in a series of advertisements. For instance, the advertisements for a restaurant may each present the following selling points, one at a time: cleanliness, quiet atmosphere, home cooking, reasonable prices, and foreign menus. There could be a temptation, for instance, to include in a toothpaste advertisement the facts that the paste prevents pyorrhea, hardens the gums, preserves the enamel, prevents decay, and sweetens the breath. To undertake the treatment of these five points in one advertisement would violate the principle of unity. If each is treated separately, however, in a series of five advertisements, the advertising will be much more effective.

Coherence means arranging the parts of the advertisement logically so that the message will be understood. The copy should be written in direct, simple language. Arguments and selling points should be stated clearly, forcefully, and convincingly. Technical terms, long words, and involved sentences should be avoided. Any sentence construction that requires study or time for comprehension should not be used. The concrete should take the place of the generality. In other words, specific details should be given. The idea suggested by the illustration should coincide with the thought expressed in the copy. Remember that the reader is at first influenced by the illustration. Good selling copy contains only vital information, is arranged in a logical order, and is written in a style that is natural and full of human interest.

Emphasis means putting stress on the most important aspect of the advertisement. The copywriter should therefore disregard all superfluous material. He should trim away all unnecessary words so that only important ones remain. He should select just those words or points that will convey the main idea to the reader. He should then put the most important words in the most conspicuous place, by means of either type or position.

Important words and sentences may be put in display type or italics, or they may be pointed out with arrows. Short sentences lend emphasis because they suggest speed, emphasize the important words, and are easy to read. At the beginning and end of an advertisement, the short sentence is particularly effective.

Point of View

The point of view from which an advertisement is read is very important. If you compare the expression "*on the market twenty-five years*" with "*in use twenty-five years*," you will find that the second expression represents the consumer's point of view. Furthermore, this expression gives the impression of service. The first expression represents the manufacturer's or dealer's point of view and suggests something to be sold rather than something of use to the buyer.

The superb ads here and on the following pages adhere to the principles of unity, coherence, and emphasis. Each ad effectively stresses one major selling point: Venture's telephone access, Frigidaire's durability, Berlitz's individual attention, Aetna's comprehensive coverage, and Kelly's varied services.

WILL HE GET MORE FOR YOUR STOLEN TV THAN YOU DO?

If you're like most homeowners, your insurance only pays the <u>depreciated</u> value of what you lose.

So before Mr. Lightfingers strikes, you should know about Ætna's remarkable Homeowners Contents Replacement Cost Coverage.

Unlike ordinary policies, this coverage replaces old property with <u>new</u>, up to four times its current value. To give you a new full-color beauty for your stolen one, instead of, say, a tummy-sized black-and-white.

Check your nearest agent in the Yellow Pages under Ætna Life & Casualty to learn in detail how we can make good on losses not just for theft, but fire, wind, hail, bursting pipes, and other risks of modern living.

For a few dollars more, you'll avoid the feeling of being robbed twice.

ÆEtna
LIFE & CASUALTY

The Ætna Casualty and Surety Company. The Standard Fire Insurance Company. Ætna Casualty & Surety Company of Illinois. Subject to deductibles. Not available in Kansas, New Hampshire, and some other states.

This ad, consisting of only two short sentences surrounded by white space, has dramatic impact.

As the advertiser, you may be interested in yourself, but your customers are interested primarily in themselves. From your own point of view, you might wish to say: "*I carry a full stock — the quality of my goods is excellent — my prices are very low.*" The customer's interests, however, will be better satisfied if you express your ideas in this way: "*You will find a wide variety here — the quality you appreciate at the price you wish to pay.*"

Which of the following expressions is more preferable to the advertiser?

Has been sold for fifty years
or
Has served housewives for fifty years

Give us a trial
or
Let us serve you regularly

Sold in 400 stores
or
Obtainable from 400 dealers

Buy a pair of comfort shoes
or
Ease your feet with comfort shoes

A coat for women of limited means
or
A coat that meets your purse halfway

Test Your Copy

In his book, *Advertising — Selling the Consumer* (Doubleday, Doran and Company, New York), John Lee Mahin gives suggestions for testing the efficiency of an advertisement before it is sent to the printer. Although some of these tests overlap one another, they may be used to estimate how carefully an advertisement has been prepared. After an advertisement has been completed, it should be considered as the work of somebody else, and the following tests should be applied to it:

1. Is the advertisement institutional? That is to say, will it appeal strongly to the group at which it is aimed, and does it represent the business reputation of the advertiser?

2. Is it natural? Does it ring true? Does it embody a personality? Does it sound like a message from a responsible member of the concern that is advertising?

3. Is it specific? Is the advertisement so general that it would be equally effective for use by another advertiser or for the sale of another article?

4. Is it timely? Does it gain interest by incorporating news of the day? "Timeliness in advertising," says Mr. Mahin, "is offering the public what it wants just when it ought to want it most."

5. Is it pertinent? Is it written with regard to the viewpoint of the prospective customer? Does it tell what benefit the purchaser will obtain?

6. Is it consistent? Does this advertisement belong in the campaign of which it is to be a part? Does it maintain the dignity of the firm that is putting it out? Is it too dignified? Does it agree with established selling plans?

7. Is it persistent? Is it distinctive because of a trademark, a style of illustration, composition, or hand lettering, or some other device for reminding the public that the advertisement is one of many issued by the advertiser?

8. Is it authoritative? Does it sound as though the advertiser believes in himself and in his goods, and as though he deserves a hearing?

9. Is it plausible? Is there even a single statement that is not likely to be accepted as the truth by a large number of the group to whom the advertisement is supposed to appeal?

10. Is it sincere? Does it have straightforward statements written in short, simple sentences? Are the illustrations accurately drawn, and the photographs clear? If there is a description, does it answer the questions that would be expected to arise?

ATTENTION AND INTEREST THROUGH HEADLINES

At the head of the copy, many advertisements have a line of display type called the *headline*. This line in bold type is often the most conspicuous part of the advertisement and is therefore the one thing that naturally catches the reader's eye in a hasty glance at the page. One or two *subheads* in smaller type are also often used in the body of the advertisement. Other layouts emphasize pictures and use headlines in less conspicuous type to tie the illustrations to the text. The headline is usually, however, the most important part of the advertisement, and the power of the advertisement often depends upon how successful the advertiser is in producing a headline that will appeal to the public. Frequently a change in the headline, without any other change in copy, will produce a successful advertisement out of an unsuccessful one.

Functions of Headlines

The purposes of a headline are:

1. To attract attention. The all-important means of attracting attention is contrast. Apart from advertising, contrast in our everyday life is what attracts our attention. When we walk through the streets and see a person of unusual height or dress, our attention is attracted because of the contrast between that person and other people. In a parade of giants or dwarfs, no one giant or dwarf would receive extra attention because of height. A small noise following a deep silence receives marked attention, whereas it might not have been noticed at all under other circumstances.

Headlines are probably the most important and most used mechanical means of attracting attention. The attention value depends on the contrast in the size of type used throughout the ad. If a whole advertisement were set in display type, the power for attracting attention would be diminished. An advertisement may carry one headline, with perhaps one or two subsidiary headlines, but beyond this point there is a danger of the advertisement losing attention value. A minor headline at the top of an advertisement, the principal headline at the optical center (just above the exact center), and a minor headline, often the name of the business concern, at the bottom make a strong and attractive layout.

2. To arouse interest. The purpose of advertising, which is to sell goods or service, is not accomplished unless the reader is carried beyond the point of attention. Interest must be aroused and sustained until desire can be developed. That is, the headline should make the reader anxious to read the advertisement so as to find out more about the product advertised.

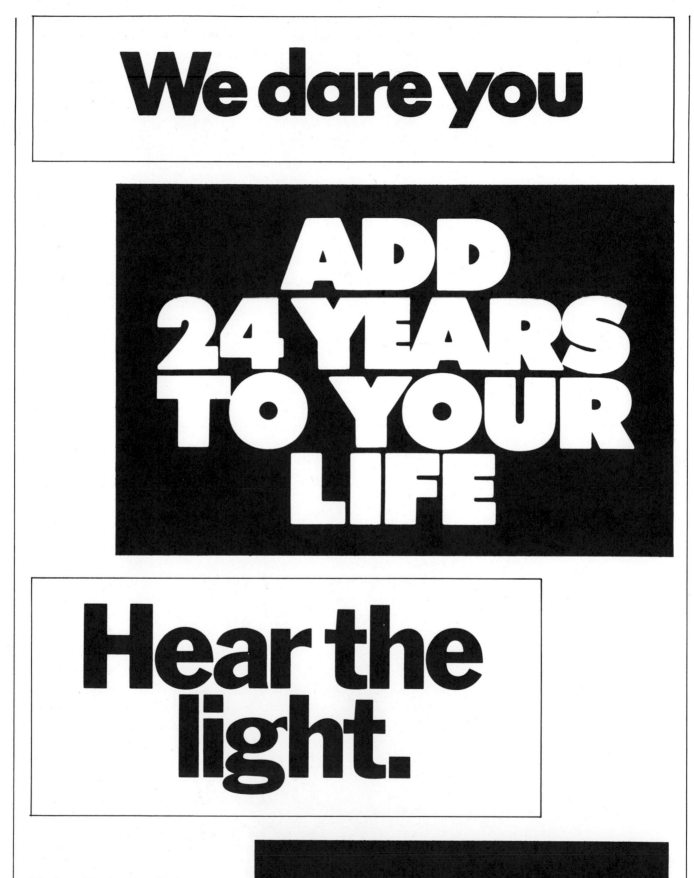

We dare you

ADD 24 YEARS TO YOUR LIFE

Hear the light.

Attention-getting headlines. Don't you wish you could see the rest of each of these ads? That's the idea!

Once you're in 'em you never want to get out

61

Care must always be exercised so that the proper balance between attention and interest is maintained. Sometimes it is advisable to sacrifice interest in order to strengthen the attention value of an advertisement. But always remember that the attention obtained must be converted into interest. The means used to gain attention and interest in the headline must also be consistent throughout the ad. Sensational, irrelevant, deceitful, humorous, or clever headlines usually do not attract attention of a kind that can easily be developed into interest.

When dramatization is used in an advertisement, the headline sets the stage for the dramatic action or serves to connect a picture with the text.

3. To make the advertisement more attractive and readable. Solid or unbroken copy is liable to appear uninteresting and forbidding. Paragraph divisions are not sufficient, however, to make the copy attractive. Sub-heads break the monotony of the composition and make the whole layout seem more inviting. They may frequently give suggestions as to the essential points covered in the text and thus help the reader to choose those parts in which he will be interested.

Content of the Headline

The mechanical makeup of the headline serves the purpose of catching the eye of the reader. The content of the headline is the factor that determines whether the reader will give the advertisement more than a passing glance.

If that momentary attention is to be prolonged and strengthened into interest, the idea expressed and the words chosen must stimulate in the reader's mind favorable thoughts and a desire to read further into the advertisement. The best headline not only gives a summary of the advertisement's text but does it in such a way as to create in the reader a desire to know more. The headline must be a condensed statement; it must be specific, all generalities having been omitted; it must be unusual, all that is commonplace having been eliminated, it must be original, perhaps breaking into the very heart of the story, it must be full of human interest; and it must appeal to the instincts in a way to compel attention.

To a large degree, the particular product or service offered in the advertisement will determine the content of the headline. When the purpose is to impress a name upon the public, the name of the product is usually the headline. In general, the national advertising of breakfast foods

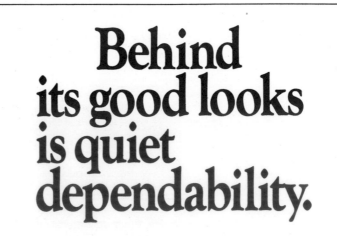

A good headline serves to summarize and preview the contents of an ad.

62

We've got your sunshine

How long does it take to unwind?

The mechanical makeup as well as the content of the headline can attract attention.

6 good reasons (and 1 super reason) why your new refrigerator should be a Kenmore.

has followed this plan in the effort to familiarize the public with the names of the various foods advertised. Sometimes the name appears in distinctive type or in a design in the form of a trademark. In some cases a slogan has been associated with a product so long that it may be used as a headline with as much distinction as the name itself.

The advertisement may emphasize the name of the business as the principal headline. The advertising of Tiffany & Company, New York, has long been of this type. Usually, though, the name of the firm is used as a subsidiary display line at the bottom of the advertisement.

Department-store advertising frequently uses price as a principal headline. This is a natural procedure when goods are sold on a price basis and when price, rather than style or service, is the important selling point.

Some headlines express a command. Examples of this type are the following:

Don't Heat All Outdoors

Build a House with Mirrors

Other headlines ask questions that tend to stimulate attention and interest in what follows.

Where Do Your Old Letters Go?

Which Fork?

What Is the Outstanding Feature of This Car?

Many headlines state a fact that may or may not have any apparent connection with the product advertised. This type of headline is especially effective when a story that is associated with the product appears in the body of the advertisement or in the illustration.

Examples of this type of headline are:

It Is a Different Laundry Now

She Loves Oats

This House Has a Disturbing Secret

The Rockefeller Fortune Owes Much of Its Growth to Sleep

How Thirteen-Year-Old Rugs Are Often Mistaken for New

Selling points may often be used as headlines — sometimes in a blunt form, and sometimes in a subtle way.

La France Saves Time, Labor, Clothes

Amazingly Delicious

New Beauty — New Comfort — Old Dependability

Luxury by Night — Beauty by Day

Warmth Aplenty

Adds to Your House of Leisure

Cold Weather Driving

Some headlines, such as the following, are purely suggestive:

When You Entertain for Dinner

Net Profits in Your Plant

Another Half-Hour of Childhood

Frequently a picture is used to gain attention, and the headline explains some feature of the picture. The Pepsodent advertisement that contains an illustration and the headline **The Danger Line** is an example of this type.

The conversational headline is often used in connection with a picture.

Nonsense, My Dear! Bring Your Rubbers in Too! Mud and Water Won't Hurt This Rug!

A change in a headline often makes an enormous difference in the number of inquiries resulting from an advertisement.

161 New Ways to Win a Man's Heart proved to be four times as effective as **A New Recipe for Home Happiness.**

Want to Get Ahead? brought nearly fifty times as many inquiries as **Beware of Spiders!**

Ship-Shape Condition, as a headline for a life-insurance advertisement, brought in many more letters than the headline **March — The Danger Month.**

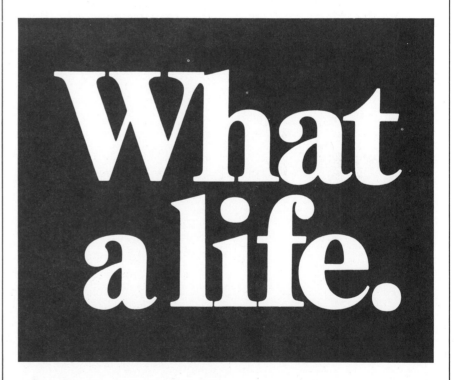

Changes in the words of these headlines might have proved disastrous.

How to get better insurance coverage on your home without increasing your premium.

Characteristics of Effective Headlines

To be effective, the headline should be concise, clear, and original. It should be made up of small words so that it may be easily comprehended, and it should be specific rather than general. The power of the eye is limited to about five words at a time; the headline, therefore, is in danger of losing some of its forcefulness if it contains many words. It should interest the reader and in some way connect the reader's experience with the goods advertised. It should use suggestion in order to draw the reader's attention to the body of the text. It should be set in type that will contrast with the rest of the printing in the advertisement as well as harmonize with the latter type.

THE KINDS OF COPY

Habits, emotions, and reasoning enter in varying degrees into the customer's decision to purchase goods. Therefore, the advertiser must be sensitive to the needs of the particular audience he is trying to reach.

Reason-Why Copy

If the advertiser wishes to appeal chiefly to reason or intellect, he uses *reason-why* or *argumentative copy*. He aims to persuade and convince by the use of facts, selling points, drawings, diagrams, and charts. Exposition and argument are used to prove the superiority of the merchandise. The advertisement becomes a written demonstration of what the article will do for the purchaser and gives logical reasons why the product should be purchased. The advertisement attempts to give the reader the necessary facts and to lead him to a decision based on due deliberation.

Human-Interest Copy

If reason were the governing principle of all action, only reason-why copy would be used in advertising. Other factors, however, are often more powerful than reason. Sympathy, anger, love, envy, and other emotional reactions are major determinants of consumer behavior. Thus, the need for *human-interest*, or *suggestive copy*.

Advertising that addresses itself chiefly to the emotions, rather than to reason or intellect, is called human-interest copy. This kind of advertising is based upon appeals to pride, fear, justice, patriotism, friendship, happiness, and other emotions to which the average person reacts.

Sense-Appeal Copy

If an advertisement makes an appeal to one or more of the five senses, it is *sense-appeal copy*. Copy that is principally descriptive and reflects the use of the product usually forms the basis of sense-appeal advertisements. Food advertisements invariably make use of sense appeal by means of an illustration and descriptive adjectives, such as *appetizing, refreshing, and delicious*. Appeals are often made to as many senses as possible (taste, touch, smell, sight, hearing) in the fundamental development of the advertisement. This form of advertising is usually a specialized type of human-interest copy.

You grow.

Puerto Rico offers you the manufacturing, transport, communication facilities you need for expansion:

- Fast start-up — 56 buildings totaling 1,163,703 sq. ft. ready for immediate occupancy, many at $1.50 per foot.
- Fifth largest port for container shipping in the world — 35% tonnage increase in the last two years.
- Second largest public utility in U.S. Energy capacity has steadily increased to 4.2 million kw with 2.2 million kw capacity in reserve.
- Air cargo lift totaled 186,180 tons in 1978, with average annual growth for the last four years of 19.4%. Twenty-one airlines serve world-wide markets.

We grow.

Increased industrial output means a higher standard of living and a more able work force:

- Manufacturing employment rose to 156,700 jobs as of October 1979.
- Upward mobility: Now over 13,000 island-trained middle managers and top professional executives.
- Manufacturing payroll increments have contributed $337,000,000 annually to other sectors of the economy.
- Advanced training programs have created a highly skilled work force capable of producing complex products like computers, pacemakers and other cardiovascular equipment.

Puerto Rico, U.S.A.
The ideal second home for American Business.

A partnership that works.

For more information: Write us on your company letterhead, Puerto Rico Economic Development Administration, Dept. BW-28, 1290 Avenue of the Americas, New York, New York 10019. Or call us, toll free (800) 223-0699 ext. 228

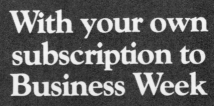

DAZZLE

Get it at your dentist regularly.

It's more than a look. It's a wonderful feeling to know your teeth are in fine shape. And the only way to be sure is by regular visits to your dentist. Get a checkup at least once a year and your teeth won't be a problem, they'll be a joy. The cost is downright cheap — less than you probably pay in a year for haircuts.

If they don't already have a dental insurance plan where you work, ask about starting one. These plans have already made it easier for over 60 million Americans to stay on a program of regular checkups.

Dazzle. When your teeth have it, you have it. So go get some at your dentist's.

The American Dental Association

Sense appeal can be created through words or, most effectively, through illustrations. Even the brightness of teeth can be simulated.

Another example of an ad that appeals to the senses.

Educational Copy

The purpose of *educational copy* is to increase public knowledge of a particular product, organization, or service. Such copy must attempt to increase familiarity with the commodity so that it will become a part of the consumer's life. The copy should be informative; it should explain the use and care of the product as well as show how to get the most value from a purchase. The information presented should be sufficiently stimulating to convert the reader into a buyer.

Testimonial Copy

Testimonial copy is of a great many kinds. When the testimonial comes from some well-known person, it has an association value, that is, it connects the product with the person. Very often, however, it is merely weak evidence of the product's value. This type of copy is not used now as much as it was. Perhaps the inundated consumer has become wary of the overly sincere celebrity.

Institutional Copy

Institutional copy aims at developing goodwill rather than selling any merchandise. By setting forth the history, the practices, or the policies of the business, it seeks to acquaint readers with facts that will place the concern high in the estimation of the buying public. Selling points are not offered, and particular products are not mentioned.

MARY HEALY HAS SOMETHING TO SING ABOUT.

Nineteen years ago, Mary Healy had a success she'll never forget: recovering from cancer. She and almost 2 million others are living proof that serious forms of cancer can be beat. But not without the research and advances in treatment that your donations help to fund. Your contributions are important. As important as life itself.

CANCER CAN BE BEAT.

American Cancer Society

Testimonials from celebrities are quite common.

MOTOROLA HELPED BRING

His name isn't important. His story is.

He was simply walking back to his office when the pain hit him.

In less than three minutes, an ambulance with two paramedics arrived.

But as they began to work, arrhythmia—erratic, wildly uncontrolled heartbeat—set in.

Then his heart stopped altogether.

A MIRACLE OF ELECTRONICS.

Fortunately, the ambulance was equipped with a Motorola APCOR Coronary Observation unit.

It put the paramedics in immediate touch with an emergency physician at the hospital miles away.

Not just by voice communication; that doesn't give a doctor all the information he needs.

But at the very same instant, by Motorola telemetry, an electrocardiogram of the activity of the man's heart was being transmitted.

A miracle of electronics—microelectronics—was about to show what it could do.

TECHNOLOGY DOES THE TALKING.

A lot of things were happening at once.

The medical assistants at the scene were talking to the emergency room at the hospital.

And the Motorola APCOR was also talking to the doctor in a language only a medical professional could understand—by transmitting the patient's EKG.

The doctor could then treat the patient almost as if he were on the spot.

In a few minutes, the man's heart began to beat. He was once again on his way to being alive, in every sense of the word.

MICROCIRCUITS MAKE IT HAPPEN.

APCOR is made possible by Motorola microcircuits, tiny information processors that transmit both electronic

THIS MAN BACK TO LIFE.

signals and the human voice.

Microcircuitry is also at the heart of the many other kinds of two-way communications equipment we make.

A microcomputer, drawn larger than life.

But communications equipment is only one of the ways in which Motorola makes electronics history.

MAKING ELECTRONICS HISTORY.

Thanks to Motorola microelectronics, we create all kinds of remarkable systems that would have been inconceivable not long ago.

A system to help power companies handle peak loads without danger of blackouts.

An electronic car-engine management system that can save gasoline.

Even a communications system that helped probe Mars.

But then, we've come a long way from the time we first made history by putting radios into cars (we went on to put alternators and electronic ignitions into them) and later put popular-priced TV sets into homes (they're a product we don't make here at all anymore).

Today, Motorola is one of the world's largest manufacturers dedicated exclusively to electronics, as well as one of its foremost designers of custom and standard semiconductors.

Many of the things we make are changing people's lives.

Others are actually saving them.

(M) MOTOROLA
Making electronics history.

APCOR, Motorola and (M) are registered trademarks of Motorola, Inc.

For further information, write Public Affairs Office, Corporate Offices, Motorola, Inc. 1303 E. Algonquin Road, Schaumburg, Illinois 60196.

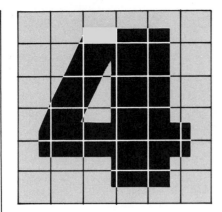

THE TYPE

How to copy-fit, select, and order suitable type styles and how to use instant lettering.

THE TYPE

If you are going to order type for your ad or other printed matter, it is essential that you speak the language of the printer or typographer, to some extent. Let us begin, therefore, with the most basic information about type.

Capital letters are usually called caps.

Lower case letters are usually two-thirds the height of the caps, though this will vary with type style.

Numerals are usually the size of caps.

The size of type is determined by the total height of the face or body including the ascenders, letter size, descenders, and the metal shoulder.

MEASUREMENTS OF TYPE

Type manufacturers have agreed upon a uniform standard of measurement called the point system. All type is made and measured in strict conformity with this standard, and the basic unit of measurement is one point, 1/72 of an inch.

Each size of type is named according to the number of points. Six-point type is therefore 6/72 of an inch. When such type is set as close as possible, there is 1/72 of an inch from the bottom of one letter to the bottom of the next line, and it is termed "set solid." Where more space between lines is required, the printer will separate the lines with a lead slug the thickness of the desired space. Most printing is done with two-point leads (pronounced *leds*).

ABCDEFGHI
8 pt.

ABCDEFGHI
10 pt.

ABCDEFGHI
12 pt.

ABCDEFGHI
14 pt.

ABCDEFGHI
18 pt.

ABCDEFGHI
24 pt.

ABCDEFGHI
30 pt.

ABCDEFGHI
36 pt.

ABCDEFGHI
42 pt.

These are variations in the point size of a most popular type style, the Caslon #540. Note that as the size increases the spread widens.

Various type sizes in common use.

The following copy, set in various type sizes in common use, shows clearly why the ten- and twelve-point type is most often used for body copy.

8 pt. type

SOLID

The highly trained type-craftsn
pography works with artwork,
d. At LIN CRAFT skilled type-cra
anging moods of modern adver
plus the skill and judgment tha

2 POINT LEADED

The highly trained type-craftsr
pography works with artwork,
d. At LIN CRAFT skilled type-cr
anging moods of modern adver

10 pt. type

SOLID

The highly trained type-cra
hat the typography works w
n that was intended. At LIN
nts needed for the pulsing, c
themselves the born artistry

2 POINT LEADED

The highly trained type-cra
hat the typography works w
n that was intended. At LIN
nts needed for the pulsing, c

12 pt. type

SOLID

The highly trained ty
d *feel* of the ad, so tha
nd copy to achieve the
CRAFT skilled type-cra
for the pulsing, chang
ve within themselves

2 POINT LEADED

The highly trained ty
d *feel* of the ad, so tha
nd copy to achieve the
CRAFT skilled type-cra
for the pulsing, chang

14 pt. type

SOLID

The highly trained
pirit and *feel* of the
work, layout, and c
was intended. At LI
eir fingertips the fo
ds of modern advert
e born artistry requ

2 POINT LEADED

The highly trained
pirit and *feel* of the
work, layout, and c
was intended. At L
eir fingertips the fo
ds of modern adver
e born artistry requ

Most type styles or *faces* are obtainable in at least three different weights, known usually as light, medium, and bold. The size and shape of any given letter is identical on all weights, but the differing thickness of the weights imparts a different feel to the letters.

Popular styles will have a greater range of weights. Note that as the weights increase fewer letters will fit into the same space, even though the point size remains the same.

Helvetica, a popular type, set in different weights.

Helvetica Thin

Helvetica Light

Helvetica

Helvetica Medium

Helvetica Medium OUTLINE

Helvetica Bold

Helvetica Bold Out.

Helvetica Ultra Black

Helvetica Light Italic

Helvetica Italic

Helvetica Italic Out.

Helvetica Medium Italic

Helvetica Medium Flair

Helvetica Bold Italic

Helvetica Reg. EXTENDED

FAMILIES OF TYPE	With literally thousands of type styles available, it is well to note that there are, in general, five major groups. Each group has many variations, yet each group has certain characteristics in common.

E1

Roman Styles

More widely used than all others, roman type styles have (1) thick and thin parts that are never varied and (2) serifs, which serve as decorative terminals on most letters.

E1a

Gothic Styles

The strokes of gothic lettering are usually of uniform thickness, but they may have thick and thin parts. The lack of serifs keeps them in the gothic family.

E1a

Italics

These letterforms are always slanted. Italic type gives emphasis to a word or line of copy when used sparingly.

Display

Script

These letters are connected as in handwriting. They may be straight up or slanted, delicate or bold.

𝕰𝕝

Text or Old English

Because its legibility is poor, this style is reserved for occasions that require an old-fashioned spirit, or for ads featuring testimonials and documents.

Examples, from top to bottom, of roman, gothic, italic, script, and text type styles.

PROPORTIONS OF TYPE

In most cases, though not always, typefaces are made in three different proportions: normal, condensed, or extended.

Obviously, these options either permit more letters to fit into a given space, or, conversely, where space and width permit, words can be extended, or if you prefer, elongated and spread out. In all cases, letters maintain the same height and basic shape.

This permits the designer greater flexibility in fitting copy into a given space with the use of either normal, condensed, or extended letters. Below we show the variations of one style, with all letters the same height, 36 points.

Franklin Gothic

ABCDEFGHIJKLMNOP
36 pt. Franklin Gothic

ABCDEFGHIJKLMNOPQRST
36 pt. Franklin Gothic Condensed

ABCDEFGHIJKLMNOPQRSTUVWXYZ
36 pt. Franklin Gothic Extra Condensed

ABCDEFGHIJKLM
36 pt. Franklin Gothic Extended

Different proportions of Franklin Gothic typefaces.

AN EXAMPLE OF ONE TYPE FAMILY

The display lines of the Bodoni family shown here are all set in 30 points. Note the variety of weights that are available in an individual family of type.

There will also be a difference in the width of each face. This requires a character count for proper copy fitting.

Bodoni

Bodoni Italic

Bodoni Bold

Bodoni Bold Italic

Bodoni Bold Condensed

Bodoni Ultra

Bodoni Ultra Italic

Bodoni Ultra Extra Condensed

Some of the different weights available for one type family, Bodoni.

80

MEASURING SPACE

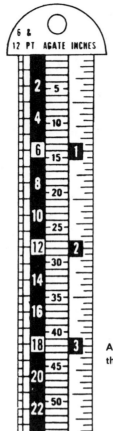

A ruler commonly used for type spacing
that measures points, agates, and inches.

The width or depth of a line of type is stated in terms of picas. There are six picas to the inch, and these may be broken down to fractions of an inch, but stated or specified as picas. A space 1" x 2" will be termed 6 x 12 picas.

The ruler shown here is available to anyone working with type and serves as an easy measure of the space that is needed for type in an ad. In newspaper advertising as well as small-space magazine ads, the depth of space is measured in terms of agate lines, of which there are fourteen to the inch.

The standard newspaper column is 2 1/16 inches (or thirteen picas wide). Magazine columns vary and here it is necessary to know the exact size for layout purposes.

When measuring type and space for copy fitting remember the following:
1. The height (size) of type is always expressed in points.
2. The width of a line of type is measured in terms of picas, always six to the inch.
3. The depth of space in which type is set is measured in agate lines, fourteen to the inch (for newspapers).

Some examples of the many type styles and weights available. Note that usually a maximum of two styles is used in any one ad.

60 pt. Baskerville

10 pt. Helvetica Light

36 pt. Baskerville

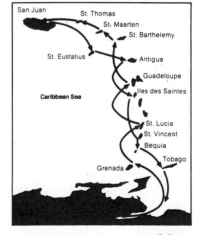

30 pt. Futura Ultra Bold Condensed

9 pt. Futura Light

36 pt. Aurora Condensed

30 pt. Aurora Condensed

9 pt. News Gothic Condensed

7 pt. News Gothic Bold

9 pt. News Gothic Condensed

24 pt. Beton Light

48 pt. Caslon Bold

84

INSTANT LETTERING

This product, in its infinite variety, is easily the most valuable, versatile, and useful tool available to the nonprofessional in making advertising material of all kinds (either singly or for reproducing in quantities), where type and/or lettering is needed.

Instant lettering refers to a pressure-sensitive dry transfer system that provides an easy and rapid method for setting high-quality type. Letters, numerals, symbols, illustrations, and tonal effects are printed onto a plastic-based film with an adhesive and by use of pressure the characters will be transposed onto almost any clean, dry surface.

A sampling of some Letraset symbols.

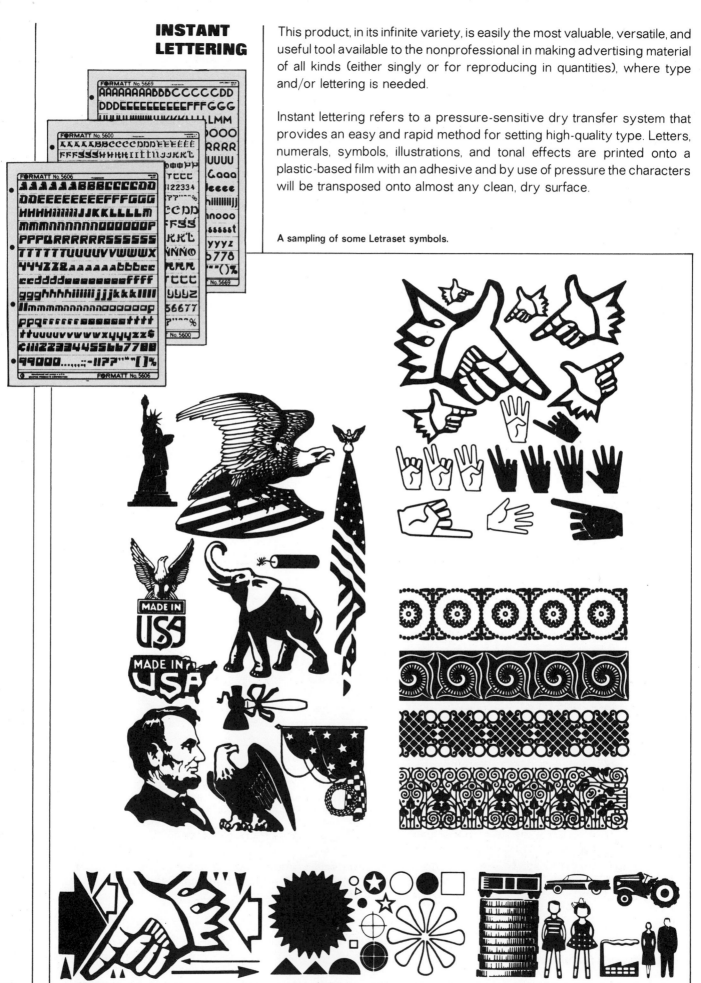

American
Typewriter Light Cond

American
Typewriter Medium Cor

American
Typewriter Bold

Aristocrat

Avant Garde
Gothic Medium C

Avant Garde
Gothic Bold Conc

Beton Bold
Condensed

Bodoni *Extra Bold*

Block *Condensed*

Capone *Medium*

Cathedral

Company

Conference

Delphin No I

ELEFONT

El Greco

Eras Bold

Flamenco Inline

Frankfurter *Medium*

Garamond *Ultra Condensed*

Gillies Gothic Bold

Graphis *Extra Bold*

Le Golf

Here is a sampling from the over 300 type styles available. There are twenty-five point sizes, from 6 to 288. All are available in black; over 100 are available in white. Helvetica Medium is also available in red, blue, green, and gold.

Easy to use, instant lettering is well worth the time, effort, and expense involved. There are many brands available in art supply stores, but we will discuss and illustrate the use of Letraset products. It is advisable to obtain a catalog from art stores so that you can become familiar with Letraset's full line as well as other brands.

How to Use Instant Lettering

Remove the protective backing tissue from the sheet and align a letter using the Spacematic guide furnished by the supplier

Press the letter onto the surface with your finger and then shade lightly over the letter. Rounded ends such as ball-points produce good results. Do not use sharp or pointed objects. Never use heavy pressure in the transfer stage. Use the same light pressure as in writing.

Carefully lift the sheet away. Letter is transferred. Repeat until the word is complete.

Cover word with protective backing tissue and burnish (rub down) hard with your finger. This is most important.

Professional results can be obtained with easy-to-use Instant Lettering.

Here are some useful hints for working with instant lettering:

1. *Surface.* Work on a clean, dry surface. Fingerprints, dust, dirt, and dampness will hinder clean work.

2. *Corrections.* When errors occur on paper or art board, letters remove easily with rubber cement pickup. On hard surfaces such as metal, glass, or plastic, lay a piece of tape over the letter or word to be removed and it will lift easily.

3. *Fixing.* When letters are to be exposed to the outdoors, apply the protective spray coating made for this purpose.

4. *Storage.* Never fold or crease instant lettering sheets. Store them flat, away from heat and humidity.

Letrasign — A Sign-Lettering System

Letrasign is a vinyl self-adhesive sign system. It has a self-spacing system that obtains balanced spacing automatically, thereby giving a professional appearance to functional and display signs. It is suitable for interior and exterior signs, on vehicles (e.g., trucks), in buildings, and for display and exhibition purposes.

Shown are the two styles available in black, white, and red, in six sizes from ⅝″ (2 cm) to 6″ (15 cm).

ABCDEFGHI
JKLMNOPQ
RSTUVWXY
Z&?!ß£$◡~⟨◦⟩⟨⟩⟨⟩

abcdefghijkl
mnopqrstuv
wxyz12345
67890;,

HELVETICA MEDIUM

ABCDEFGHIJK
LMNOPQRSTU
VWXYZ&?ß!£$
◡~◟⟨◦⟩~⟨⟩⟨⟩

abcdefghijklm
nopqrstuvwxy
z1234567890

FRANKLIN GOTHIC EXTRA
CONDENSED

Even the nonprofessional can quickly
learn the Letrasign system.

The Wrico System — Good Lettering Without Skill

Not all lettering is done by the professional. Much useful lettering can be done by the layman equipped with the proper tools and a few simple instructions.

One such tool is the Wrico Lettering System, which basically consists of a special mechanical or fountain pen and a set of lettering guides. It requires neither skill nor experience to use these lettering guides effectively.

Each is a strip of Pyralin, with a series of openings so designed that when the point of a Wrico pen is moved around the sides of the openings, letters and numerals are formed. This is a useful tool for preparing signs and posters for schools, churches, and stores. Neat, clean lettering is produced with a minimum of fuss and expense.

There are limitations, of course. There is not a great variety of lettering styles and sizes to choose from. Colored inks may not be used on dark surfaces. Still, much useful work can be done with this method by amateurs and nonprofessionals.

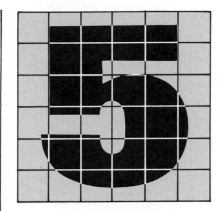

THE ILLUSTRATION

How and where to obtain illustrations
for your ad

THE ILLUSTRATION

Illustrations are no longer a luxury in an advertisement but a primary force in its effectiveness. This could easily be the stumbling block for those nonprofessionals who may wish to use an illustration but feel they do not have either the ability to produce one themselves, or the budget to have one made-to-order.

It is important, therefore, for the nonprofessional to know that, at very small cost, first-rate black-and-white drawings are available in almost any subject matter he may require.

Many of the illustrations and other symbols shown on the following pages are obtainable on dry transfer sheets, 10″ x 15″ (25 x 38 cm), with a number of them on each sheet. Adhesive-backed, they are easily applied to any layout or pasteup, ready for reproduction. They are made by Letraset U.S.A., Bergenfield, New Jersey, and are available at most art supply stores, where you can obtain catalogs showing a full range of illustrations, symbols, and alphabets.

Since any ad is enlivened by an illustration, you should try, if possible, to include an illustration in your layout design. Bear in mind that drawings are costly if you order one from an illustrator. A photographic illustration can prove to be even more costly. If the product you are advertising requires specific detail, only then should you consider a photograph. However, before you engage a commercial photographer, ask him if he has in his files an existing photo that will serve your purpose. He may well have one, and you will save a great deal.

Similarly, should you wish to go to the trouble and expense of having a drawing made to your order, find in your business directory an illustrator who specializes in the subject you require. Here again, ask for previously used drawings that may serve your purpose.

Included here is a general assortment of illustrations that you can copy directly from these pages. These drawings will serve very well for most purposes, and they may be enlarged or reduced to fit on your layout design. More may be obtained from the Letraset catalog.

WAYS TO USE ILLUSTRATIONS

Black-and-white illustrations, either photos or drawings, lend themselves to a variety of uses, with little trouble or expense.

The first consideration, after suitability, is size. The illustration must fit the space allotted to it on your layout.

This drawing would be suitable for a variety of purposes and for many products or services.

A positive (black on white) and its negative (white on black).

Simple Reduction or Enlargement

By marking off a line on the longest side of an illustration and specifying the size or length you wish, any photostat house will supply you with a duplicate of your picture. Request a *positive* if you wish another black on white. Should you wish a reverse (white on black), ask for a *negative*. Either one will be printed on heavy paper that can then be pasted down. A *glossy* print will reproduce better than a *matte* since the black is more intense.

In like manner, and by specifying the size you wish, an enlargement may be ordered.

There are many pictures within this picture; each serves a different purpose.

crop line

Cropping

This is a simple yet important device by which you focus attention on that portion of the illustration you think is important for your purpose, and frame out the rest.

There are many *shots* or pictures within any one picture, and each one will look different by changing its proportions, making it longer, wider, higher, or narrower.

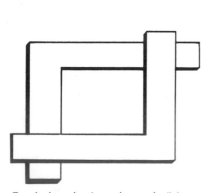

Two L-shaped strips to locate the "picture within the picture" that you need.

Cut two L-shaped strips of card, and by positioning them (as shown) and moving them around on your picture, you will obtain different views, sizes, and shapes. After you have decided on the area you wish, draw lines around the area, and have stats made. You can easily cut the area away from the rest to paste down.

Musical instruments.

Miscellaneous figures.

Miscellaneous outdoor scenes.

City and country scenes.

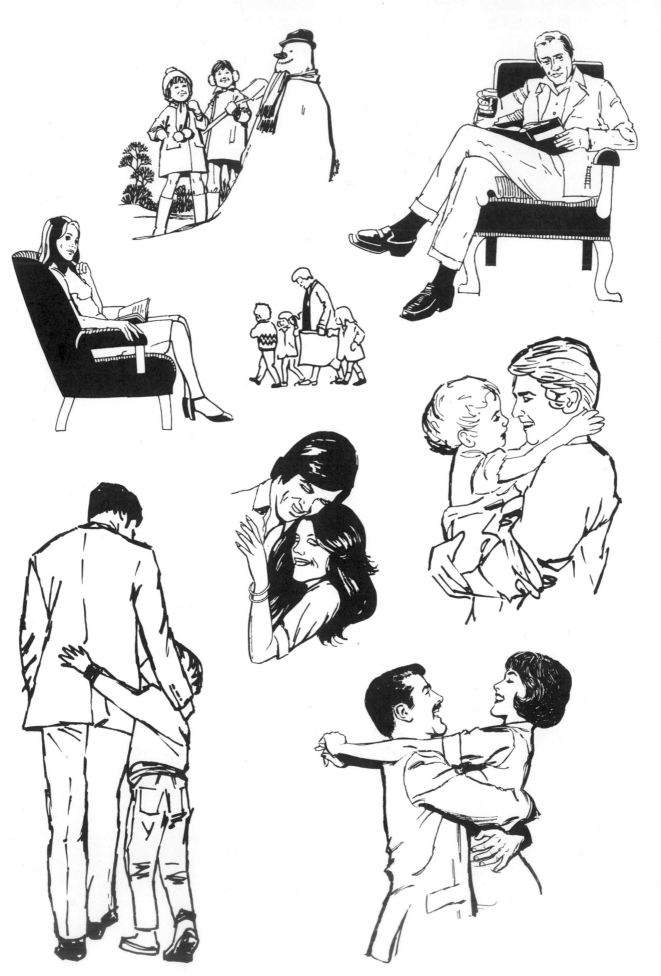

Family groups.

Holiday symbols.

Groups and crowds.

Recreational scenes.

103   Action sports.

Children of various ages.

Women in various roles.

Cartoon figures.

Animals and wildlife.

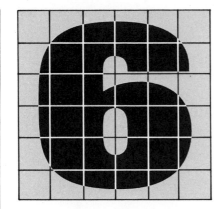

THE LAYOUT

How to arrange your copy and illustration to attract and hold attention

THE LAYOUT

The first step in creating the design or layout of your ad is to group all elements into like units. It will be much easier to design and sketch a layout if you think of these units as separate parts of the ad, to be brought together in an effective and harmonious whole.

These units would be (1) the heading — the most important part of the copy; (2) the illustration; (3) the body copy — the smaller follow-up reading matter; and (4) the signature, trademark, or logo, as it is professionally known.

Some ads may omit one or even two of these units. Others may contain more than one of them. This would be noted from the start, before any designing is done.

This is excellent integration of the major advertising units: heading, body copy, illustration, and logo.

Le Perigord, a superb French restaurant, recommends a superb French restaurant.

Le Perigord recommends Le Perigord Park. Both are equally elegant and classically French. With the same distinctive dishes of the Perigord region. Try the Canard Flambé au Grand Marnier, or the pigeon aux olives. And complement your meal with a fine wine from the distinguished wine list. Then finish up with a fluffy chocolate mousse.

Service is impeccable and the ambience at Les Perigords is as flawlessly French as is the menu. Use the American Express® Card at Le Perigord, 405 E. 52nd St., PL 5-6244; or Le Perigord Park, Park Ave. at 63rd St., 752-0050.

The American Express Card. Don't leave home without it. SM

BEGINNING THE LAYOUT DESIGN

No professional layout designer will ever attempt to make a finished or final layout design in one step. Rather, he will arrive at the final design by a series of steps or sketches, changing and improving on each as it develops from first to last stage. Each step serves a specific purpose and is described below.

1. *Make a Thumbnail Sketch.* So-called because it is quite small, about 1½" x 2", a thumbnail sketch is a miniature of the full-size ad. The sketch is made rapidly with a dark pencil or a pointed marker. It should indicate the arrangement of the various units — the heading, the illustration, the body copy, and the logo.

Begin by drawing an outline of the *full* space to be used for the ad. Then, as illustrated, extend a diagonal line from the lower left-hand corner to the upper right-hand corner. Any two horizontal and perpendicular lines that meet on the diagonal give a space which is in exact proportion to the full space. Mark off a space about 2" high, draw the connecting lines across and down, and you have a space for the thumbnail sketch. Trace over this area so that you can make five or six thumbnail sketches.

The thumbnail sketch.

Full size space and smaller proportional space.

An exact proportional reduction of the full size space to thumbnail size.

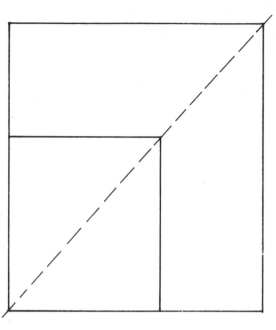

2. *Indicate the Unit Parts of the Thumbnail Sketch.* Make a number of thumbnail sketches until one suits you. Sketch them fast and rough, just good enough to recognize each unit. Use the shorthand technique of the pros as illustrated. Use a flattened pencil or marker.

Indicate the *heading* with series of spirals or connected perpendiculars of various lengths, drawn easily and rapidly, to simulate the words in the heading or main copy.

The first and quick thumbnail sketch of the heading.

The second, somewhat finer sketch of the heading.

Roughly draw in the *illustration* with no detail to show approximate size and position.

The *minor copy* is indicated by single lines, freely drawn on thumbnail (with a T-square on later sketches), showing the area to be occupied by the type.

The roughly drawn illustration.

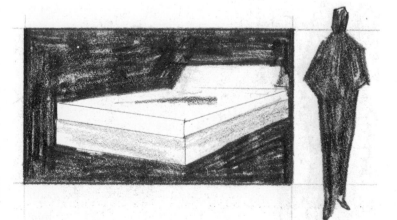

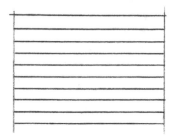

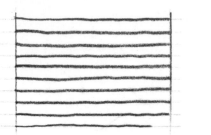

Thumbnail sketches of the minor copy.

Show the *logo or trademark* only by size and shape.

3. *Enlarge and Duplicate This Sketch to the Full Size.* Do not try to improve on the sketch. At this point, the important thing is to show the approximate space each unit will occupy on the full-size ad.

A sketch of the logo or trademark.

Alternate sketches of the full ad to determine the approximate space for each unit.

This step is especially important for beginners who have not yet developed an ability to visualize. This will carry your layout one step further.

4. *Size the Units of the Layout.* Before you can carry your sketch another step toward printing, you need to know the exact dimensions of each unit. This enables you to order these units from the printer and other specialists who will prepare them in finished form for printing.

Place a sheet of tracing paper over your full-size sketch and outline the area each unit will occupy. You will then have the exact size of each unit.

5. *Order the Heading.* Since you now know the dimensions of the space to be used in the heading, select the style and size of type that is suitable for your ad (see Chapter 4). Give this order to your printer or typographer who will set it up accordingly and supply you with a finished proof. A proof is a sheet of white paper with the reading matter printed to your specifications and subject to your review.

An enlargement of the sketch of the full ad.

6. *Order the Minor Copy.* This becomes a very difficult task for the nonprofessional. The simplest way to handle this is to supply your printer with the copy and the dimensions of the space to be used. He can then determine the exact size of the type. You are playing it safe if you ask for the same family of type used in the heading.

7. *Order the Illustration.* You may find an illustration suitable for your purposes in Chapter 5. Should you require something not available in this reference material, you will have to find a commercial artist who renders illustrations on a free-lance basis. Ask your printer to refer you or seek one out in a redbook directory. Show the artist your layout for dimensions and explain what you have in mind. You may wish to use a photograph. If so, consult a commercial photographer who may have something on hand you can use.

Whichever you use, have the specialist come up with a picture that fits the dimensions on your layout.

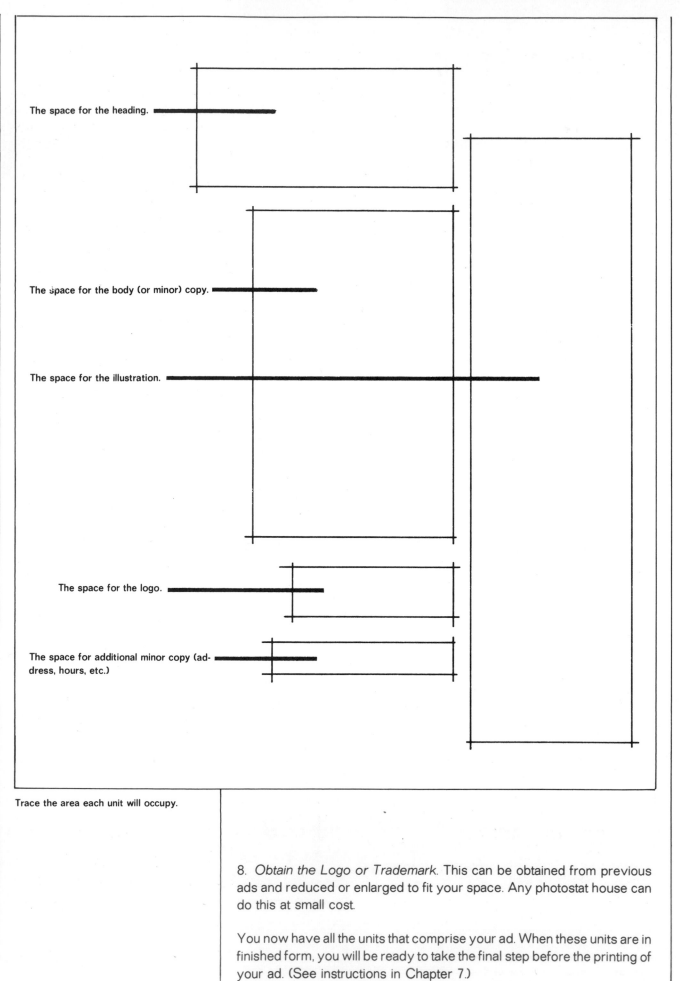

The space for the heading.

The space for the body (or minor) copy.

The space for the illustration.

The space for the logo.

The space for additional minor copy (address, hours, etc.)

Trace the area each unit will occupy.

8. *Obtain the Logo or Trademark.* This can be obtained from previous ads and reduced or enlarged to fit your space. Any photostat house can do this at small cost.

You now have all the units that comprise your ad. When these units are in finished form, you will be ready to take the final step before the printing of your ad. (See instructions in Chapter 7.)

The heading.

Informal modeling today, 12:30 till 2:30, Fifth Avenue store. See new fluid knits in topaz, a lush shimmery brown. Sparkle your day-into-evening dresses, all touched with soft beige mock suede. Obi-sashed one-piece, 8 to 16, 68.00. Knitwear, third floor, Fifth Avenue, branches.

The minor copy.

Consult Chapter 5 for ready-to-copy illustrations before looking elsewhere.

The logo can be the name of the firm or its product and can either be spelled out or represented through an illustration.

THE PRINCIPLES OF ADVERTISING DESIGN

Regardless of the differences between people, you may assume that most people react similarly to certain basic messages. Any good salesman knows this and manipulates his prospect accordingly. Likewise, a designer will make use of certain shapes and patterns that can be counted on to impress a reader favorably. Just as important, people avoid those messages that produce boredom, apathy, impatience, or confusion.

Without attempting here to cover all of the complex factors of good design, we shall deal with several major points that will guide you in making an effective design or layout.

Contrast and Ways to Achieve It

Contrast in an ad simply means the avoidance of monotony. By using one or more of the devices shown, we make our ad lively and more interesting to the reader.

The combination of the vertical illustration with horizontal lines of copy adds dynamic interest and avoids monotony.

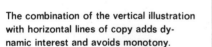

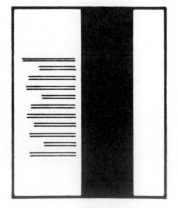

Fifth Avenue store, of our new Kimberly Knits in wool; it's got life. Shown, hood/cowl-collared fine gauge wool knit in predominantly oatmeal, black or berry stripes, leather sashed. 6 to 14. 110.00 Meadowbrook third floor, Fifth Avenue (212) MU9-7000 and branches

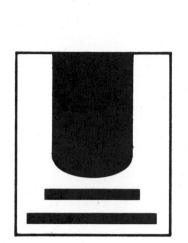

This is a small but powerful layout because of the intersecting vertical and horizontal lines.

The white wine that graces any table.

The curved lines added to the horizontals attract attention, although too much copy can hurt legibility.

4 Week Instructional Clinics For Men and Women
Beginning Tues., Sept. 21, 12 noon-1 P.M., Wed. Sept. 22, 4-5 P.M., Thurs. Sept. 23, 6:30-7:30 P.M., and Sat. Oct. 2, 10-11 A.M. Clinic fee $35.00. Equipment provided. For reservations call (212) 594-3120.

Facilities include 7 regulation-singles squash courts, pro shop, lounge, saunas and changing rooms. Open 7 days a week. $25.00 annual membership. Low court fees.

Fifth Avenue Racquet Club
404 5th Avenue, New York City

The heading has dramatic force because of its sharp angle against the verticals and horizontals.

A combination of verticals, horizontals, and diagonals makes this small ad arresting.

Parc
Swim & Health Club

Swim-o-phobia Cured

Daytime Special $169.00
Giant 60ft. Heated Pool
Open 7 Days a Week
Credit Cards Accepted
Brochure w/Rates
Available

363 w. 56th st.
Off Columbus Circle
JU•6•3675

The heading in this ad has been exaggerated in contrast to the other units. Note, also, the absence of an illustration, again in deference to the heading. Through contrast in size we have a powerful ad, forcefully presented. Do you have a dramatic and stimulating message? If so, then by all means feature the heading.

STEP UP . . .
TO THE NEW
LEATHER
DRESS BOOT

This ad is not very large, being three columns wide by only half the length of the newspaper page. Yet it appears tremendous in size and impossible to pass by without noticing the aim of every advertiser. This is achieved by devoting four-fifths of the space to the illustration, with the copy very small by comparison. This can be effective if the product has such a wide appeal that there is no harm in having the heading and copy become incidental. Note that the name of the store is featured larger and bolder than the heading.

FRANKLIN SIMON

Contrast of Color

Color in advertising does not have to be red, yellow, blue, etc. Black and white are highly visible colors, and, when effectively used, can be as powerful as any other color. Also, they are more economical.

When we print an ad with black ink on a white surface, we may also use the reverse — white on black. Also, any shade of gray may be used together with black and white, and the printing is still black and white. This will be discussed in detail later.

Some of the many interchangeable effects possible through the use of contrast of color.

120

The Use of White Space

Nonprofessionals (and for that matter, some pros who should know better) have a tendency to crowd a layout by putting too much into it or making the units too large for the space.

The white space in an ad is a positive factor and serves several important functions. It can separate the ad from adjoining ones. By presenting an uncluttered appearance, it also makes an ad easier to look at and read.

For minimum legibility there should be no less than 10 percent blank space in an ad and 20 percent is even better.

Each of the designs has almost 50 percent white space and is easier to read because of it.

THE WYKEHAM DIFFERENCE

Tucked into a lovely New England village,
Wykeham offers the warmth of a small school,
the cultural advantages of a unique and
truly outstanding program in the
creative and performing arts,
and the benefits of strong college preparatory
academics with an exceptional range
of course options. Through cooperation
with a nearby private school for boys,
many courses and activities are co-educational.
With a balanced involvement in academics,
arts and athletics, Wykeham girls (grades 9-12)
develop a keen sense of personal direction,
independence and confidence.
For catalog, write or phone:

Director of Admissions
Wykeham Rise
Washington, CT 06793
Tel. 203/868-7347

Note these examples of effective use of white space.

THE MOST DISTINGUISHED ADDRESS IN THE WORLD

Perhaps it can be yours

EMPIRE STATE

350 Fifth Avenue

Managed by
HELMSLEY SPEAR, INC.
For information call
736-3100

There is a splendid hotel on a marvelous corner of Park Avenue
where everything's coming up roses and crystal and gilt.

That hotel has earned the accolade: "One of the 300 best hotels in the world" in the new
hotel guide from Thomas Cook, London. And that's not just splendid, it's splendiferous.

Loews Drake

Contrast of line (circle and horizontal type) and much white space make this ad interesting and easy to read. It carries with it an air of casual elegance and much prestige for its sponsor.

Listen to the Good Sports

Yankees, Nets, Islanders, NFL/College Football, The John Sterling Sports Call-in

ẄMCA Radio 57
Real People Radio

The sharp contrast of black on white and white on black, by the effective use of reverse color, is dramatic. This effect is easy to achieve, is very economical, and is explained later in Chapter 7.

The Visual Flow

We read from left-to-right and top-to-bottom. With this in mind, try to arrange the units of your ad so that the eye will travel readily from unit to unit with ease, thus grasping and reading the ad without difficulty.

The layout here has to be an example of the simplest and most powerful device in layout design. The heading is at visual center (slightly above actual center), and rivets the eye first. Our reading habit carries us across to the illustration, and down to the minor copy, which is then read easily because of its position in the layout.

Rare taste.

We found a way to bottle it.

A simple yet powerful layout design.

Stanley Boxer

André Emmerich
41 E 57

The loose border design makes a prominent ad.

TEN APPROACHES TO THE DECORATIVE

Valerie Jaudon
        Arlene Slavin
Jane Kaufman
        George Sugarman
Joyce Kozloff
        John Torreano
Tony Robbin
        Robert Zakanych
Miriam Schapiro
        Barbara Zucker

September 25 - October 19, 1976

Alessandra Gallery
489 Broome Street, NYC   925-7373

Too much copy in a given space is difficult to read.

Blum Helman
13 EAST 75   TUES-SAT 10-6

Frank Stella
PAINTINGS

The use of gray, black, and white adds an interesting dimension.

124

**Pioneer
Photographers
of Brazil:
1840-1920**

SEPT. 15-NOV. 14
TUES. THRU SUN.
NOON TO 6PM

Center for
Inter-American Relations
680 Park Avenue

Type set flush left with open spacing can
be effective.

**SCULPTURE
CENTER**

**12 JAPANESE
SCULPTORS**

Thru Oct. 6

167 EAST 69 ST.
Tues-Sat from 11 to 5

This tiny ad is pleasing to the eye and has
an uncrowded look.

Lotte
Jacobi
PHOTOGRAPHS
Kimmel
Cohn
41 CENTRAL PARK WEST/64TH
TUES-SAT. 11-6   799-6675

Reverse color, used alone, adds to the
strength of this ad.

A variety of small ads (shown actual size) are presented below. This size
ad is a challenge to the designer.

WATERCOLORS & DRAWINGS
BURCHFIELD ● BURLIAK
HARTLEY ● LUKX
RIVERA ● SOYER
S'TELLA & Etc.
thru OCT. 23
SUMMIT GALLERY
101 W. 57th St.   Suite 2D
586-6734
*Tues.-Sat. 1-5 P.M.
and by appointment*

Much copy, but there is also white space
on top, bottom, and on sides to aid
legibility.

**ROY
WITLIN**

paintings
on
plexiglas

arras
29 west 57 st.

This is strong, clear, and easy-to-read because of open areas.

Pappagallo's
**LITTLE
KID**

You'll love "Paco", our
high-spirited, flat-heeled classic.
Mahogany, amber, navy or
black kid. 27.00 in our
sixth floor Shop
for Pappagallo.

B Altman & Co

Easy-to-read because of the natural flow
from top left to bottom right.

Here are more examples of visual flow.

The use of diagonals and horizontals.

WIDE·CALF BOOTS

tree·mark

The line of the boot draws the eye to the store name.

A GIANT STEP FOR MANKIND.

Gift Certificates Available

style 200 natural glove sand suede
$39.50

KALSO earth SHOE

You can buy the Earth® Brand Shoe only at an Earth® Shoe Store.

Earth® Shoe Stores

The Earth® Shoe is available only at the following locations in the New York area:
NEW YORK, N.Y.: 117 EAST 17th STREET / 793 LEXINGTON AVENUE (AT 62nd)
WHITE PLAINS, N.Y.: 108 MAMARONECK AVENUE
ROOSEVELT FIELD, L.I.: LE PETIT MALL

The visual flow in this ad is irresistible. Note the three-dimensional appearance of the illustration.

This gem of an ad has simplicity and power. It uses symbolism to present a message with artistry and subtlety. The sea, suggesting great distance, and the white on black for night combine to exert an almost hypnotic spell on the reader. The brief heading evokes a strong feeling of friendly yet powerful persuasion. Rarely do we find such a successful combination of design, artwork, copy, etc., in a single ad.

Come on over

Wherever in the world you have family and friends, wherever in the world you do business, an International telephone call is the next best thing to being there.

Similarly, the eye pull here is unmistakable and powerful.

This is almost like looking at a menu.

This reflects a novel and exotic mood.

Here there is a nautical spirit.

One can feel the Latin rhythm of this edge trim.

The Use of Borders and Panels

To most people a border is a trim or decoration. Not so in advertising layout. An ad with a border properly used can have the impact of an unbordered ad twice the size. The border serves not only to separate the ad from its surroundings, but more importantly, focuses attention on what is within its borders. When this is accomplished, it is well worth the space it takes, even when it means a reduction in size of type.

The border also has its decorative aspect. As such, it can impart a spirit or flavor that greatly enhances the entire ad.

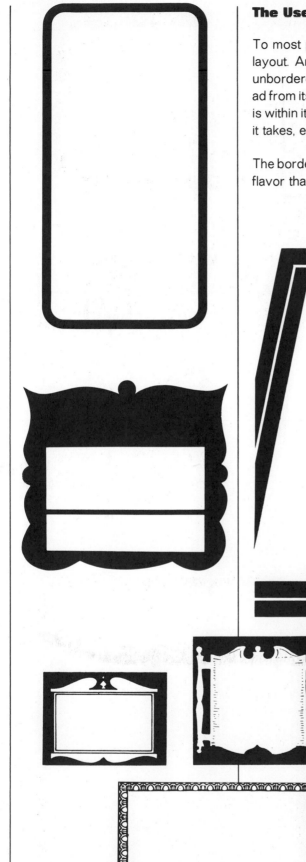

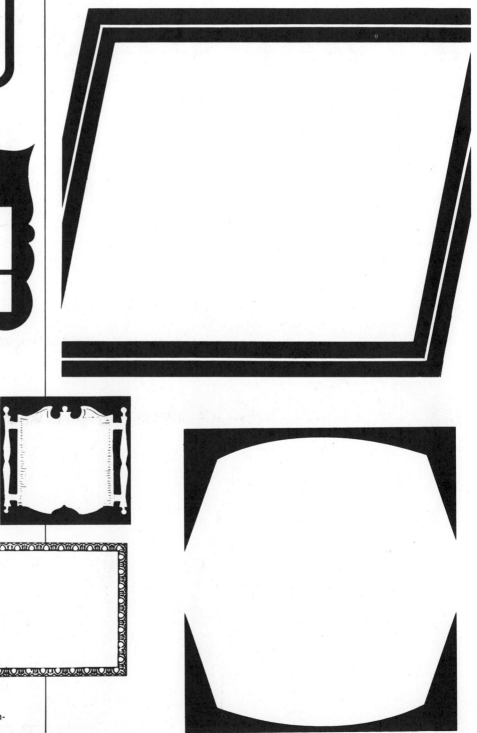

These borders may be reduced or enlarged to fit any size required.

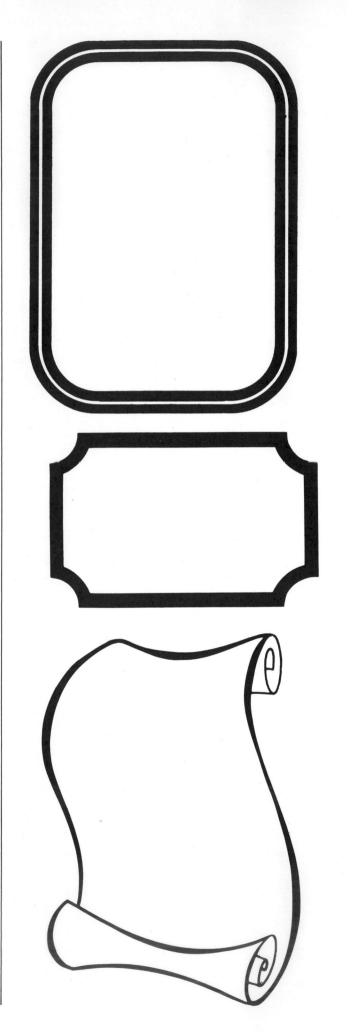

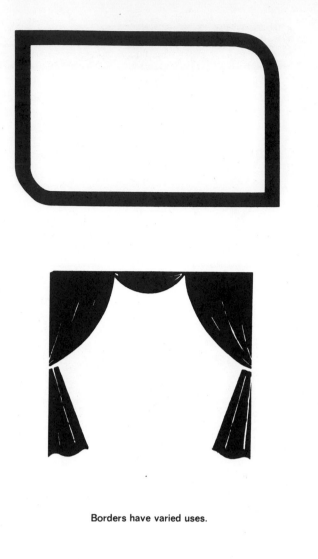

Borders have varied uses.

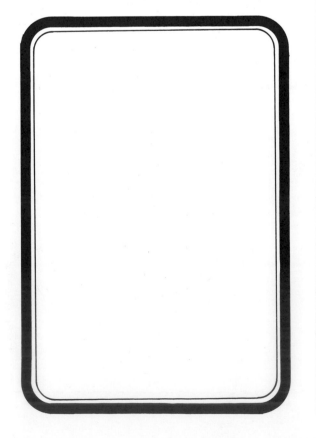

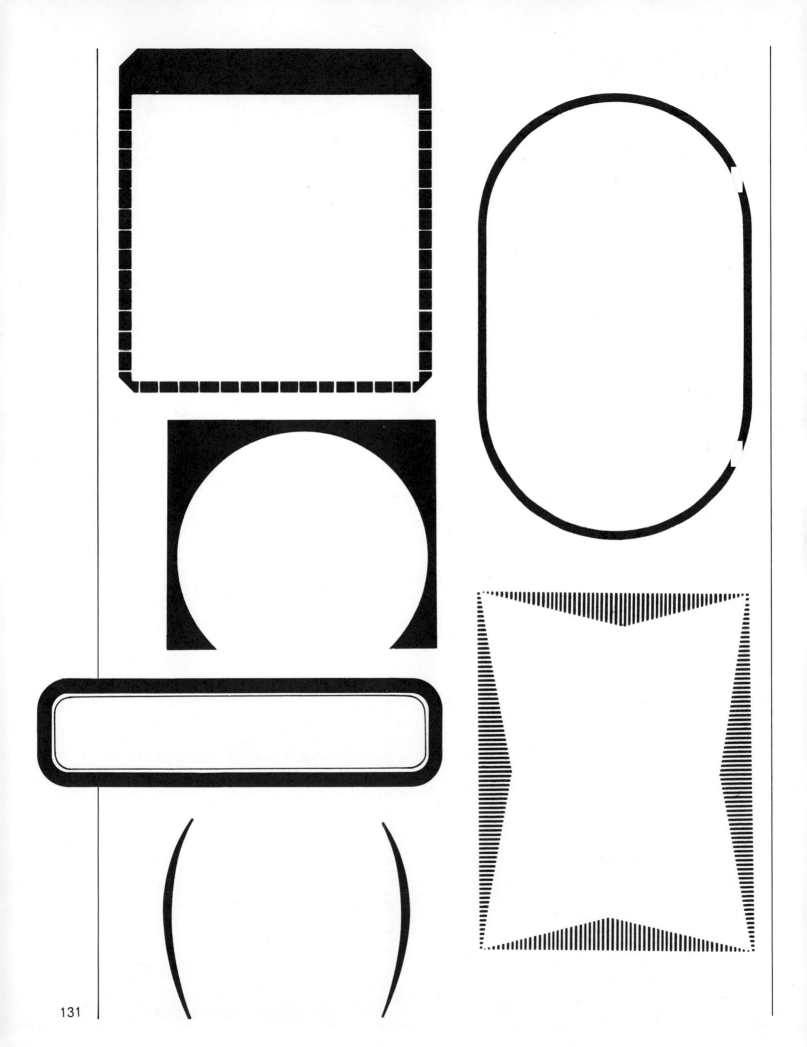

Decorative panels are used for special occasions.

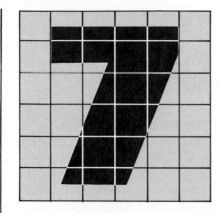

THE PASTEUP

How to prepare your ad for the printer

THE PASTEUP

WHAT IS THE MECHANICAL?

You have decided on the media for your ad, be it newspaper, magazine, direct mail, or any other that will require printing. You have determined the exact size, you have written the copy, you have made the layout design, and you have obtained the illustration you will use. You have ordered and received the type proofs, both heading and body copy. You are now ready for the final step in preparing your ad for printing. This is the making of the *mechanical*, which will be converted into the actual plate that is used by the printer for the printing of your ad.

Briefly stated, the mechanical, or pasteup as it is usually called, is a sheet of illustration board on which are assembled all the various parts of your ad according to the original design or layout. The photoengraver will convert this mechanical to a metal plate. This step, while not beyond your abilities, must be done carefully and accurately, since the printed ad will be no better than its mechanical.

You must become aware of the purpose of this final step and check your work carefully. You are now working not to suit yourself, but to measure up to the standards of the photoengraver's camera. What may appear acceptable to the naked eye may be inaccurate and downright messy to the camera's eye. And, strangely enough, what is messy to the eye, such as the varying tones of white comprising the illustration board, the type proofs, and the retouching — with blue and red lines used as guides —may be perfectly acceptable to the camera and result in a perfect plate.

Great Last Act!

The heading.

The illustration.

The various units in finished form are ready to be assembled on the mechanical.

Splendid Supper at the Algonquin. Drinks. Or simply a scrumptious selection from our Dessert Buffet.

The body copy.

THE Algonquin

The logo.

Maitre d': Robert

59 W. 44th St., New York • MU 7-4400
Complimentary garage parking all evening (5:30 p.m. to 2 a.m.) for Algonquin pre-theatre Dinner Guests.

The minor copy.

All this, then, throws the responsibility of doing a satisfactory job where it belongs — on your shoulders. Is it easy? No one says it is. Is it difficult? Only if you are all thumbs and have difficulty concentrating and following directions. Can you do it and do it well? Decidedly yes. It is your motivation, not your ability, that will be tested. Hundreds of students, some as young as sixteen, attempt this work for the first time and produce very acceptable jobs.

GETTING TO WORK

You will need most of the tools and materials listed in Chapter 6 on Layout. They are referred to as the need arises, and it is assumed you have them available.

The original design in layout form.

The pasteup is assembled on the mechanical with each unit in place.

Here is the completed ad as it appeared when printed, with border added.

135

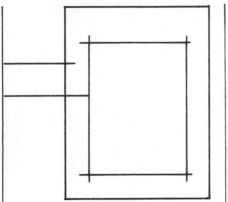

Step 1, a and b.

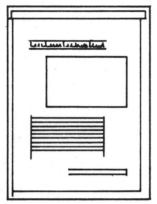

Step 1, c.

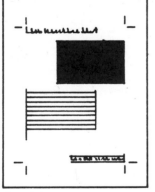

Step 1, f.

Step 1. The Preparation

a. Obtain a sheet of smooth illustration board, larger than the outside dimensions of your layout by at least 4″ (10 cm) on all four sides.

b. On this board, using a well-sharpened light blue pencil, draw lines indicating the outside area of the layout. These lines may cross at corners. Remember that light blue does not reproduce under the camera when the plate is made, and so may be used for all guidelines on the face of the board.

c. Now fasten your original full size layout sketch to another board with masking tape. This layout will serve as a working guide for making the mechanical.

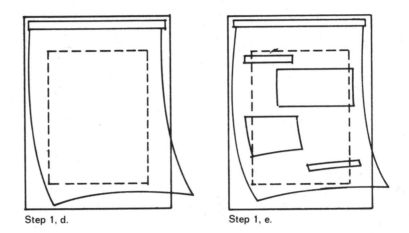

Step 1, d.   Step 1, e.

d. Make an overlay on this original layout by placing over it a sheet of tracing paper, larger than the layout, and attaching it with masking tape on four sides to the surface of the board.

e. On this tracing paper overlay (and this is important), with an HB sharpened pencil, draw an outline of the area occupied by each unit —heading, illustration, body copy, logo, etc. Use the T-square for horizontals, and the triangle for the perpendiculars by resting it on the top edge of the T-square. We are interested in squaring up the space or area of each separate unit. This will help you position these units on the mechanical, according to their place on the original layout.

f. Now, assemble all of the finished units that are parts of the layout, checking each one for cleanliness, accuracy, and the print-readiness of the black. If any unit is not the actual size called for on the layout, you must have it reduced or enlarged photostatically (see notes on Photostats, this chapter).

Step 2. The Pasteup

Now proceed to position and paste down each unit in your ad, according to the measurements on the overlay.

It's better

136

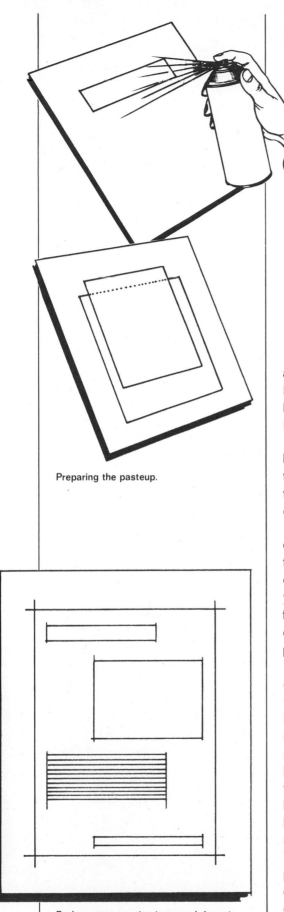

Preparing the pasteup.

Each pasteup section is pasted down in its appropriate position.

a. Start with the heading. Take this section of the printed proof, and with a light blue pencil, draw the same area lines as on the overlay. Extend each blue line outward about ½″ (1 cm). Use T-square and triangle as before. Measure accurately from outside border line.

b. Using a sharp single-edge razor blade, cut the heading section from the proof sheet, allowing an extra ¼″ (.63 cm) margin. The blue lines on this section will be sharp and clean against the edge of the section, enabling you to match them up with the blue lines on the board itself.

c. Place this section face down on a clean surface. Apply rubber cement to the back side. If you use one coat of rubber cement you can avoid coating the face of the board. Spray adhesive will also serve here, but if you do use this spray, be very certain to work near ventilation since the fumes are toxic and must be avoided. Keep a distance of at least 18″ (46 cm). In either case, allow the cement to dry for several minutes before pasting down. Check it and if it looks wet, allow more drying.

d. Now, hold the section with an ordinary tweezer in your left hand and with the thumb and forefinger of your right hand. Bring the section to the board and match up the blue guidelines on the top side. Mount the section onto the surface of the board by allowing ½″ (1 cm) of the top edge of the section to adhere while keeping the rest of the piece tilted up, clear of the board. As your right hand becomes free, take a piece of card or edge of the triangle and smooth out the section from top to bottom. If the piece being mounted is large and unwieldy, insert a waxed sheet of paper between the piece and the board, up to within a ½″ (1 cm) of top line. Then slide the waxed sheet out as you lower the cemented section gradually. This is called slip-sheeting and will prevent premature adhering. Press the piece into position, using the edge of the triangle. Then place a clean sheet over the area and rub firmly. Now lift the paper and check your work closely.

e. The section should now be pasted down in position, smooth, flat, and clean. Use the T-square to check alignment. Some pasteup workers will now paint the edges of the mounted section with poster white using a small brush. This serves to eliminate smudges too faint to the naked eye and also tends to reveal particles of cement left over for cleaning. You will now have what seems like a messy business with whites of board, proof, and paint — all different tones to the eye. However, under the platemaker's camera all will show as one white.

f. Remove all particles of rubber cement with a rubber cement pickup or soft eraser. Bear in mind that printer's ink never dries hard and smudges easily when rubbed. Check carefully for finger marks and alignment of type. You are now ready to proceed mounting the other parts of the layout in similar fashion.

TO PRINT A SECOND COLOR AT NO EXTRA COST

So far, we have described the handling of a mechanical intended for printing in a single color with no tints or tones, as in a wash illustration or a photograph. Such a plate is termed a linecut, which means that everything in the ad is to be printed in a single solid color on a white or colored paper.

Regardless of the final color used in the printing (and it may be any color ink), the preparation will be a simple black on white pasteup of each unit in the layout. As stated before, this "mechanical" is converted by the photoengraver into a linecut plate which the printer will use to print any one single solid color on the selected surface.

Different effects can be obtained in one-color printing. Shown here are a black-on-white and a white-on-black ad section. By using tints, you can introduce various shades of gray at no additional cost.

An example of a linecut.

Let's consider a simple variation of the single color. You may incorporate a tint of your chosen color that will give the effect of a second color, at no added cost to the advertiser beyond the cost of preparing the mechanical. For example, if you are printing with black ink, you can use a gray for large headings, on the illustration, or as background area. Or, if you are using red ink for printing, you may use any shade of pink (a tint of the red) on any part of the job. To obtain this added color tone, you must prepare the mechanical pasteup for it.

Preparation of a Color Tint

When a solid area of any color is broken down into dots of the same color and printed, the visual effect is that of a lighter tone of that color. To be more accurate, the lighter tone is achieved by the white spaces between

Solid black can appear any shade of gray simply with the use of a tint.

138

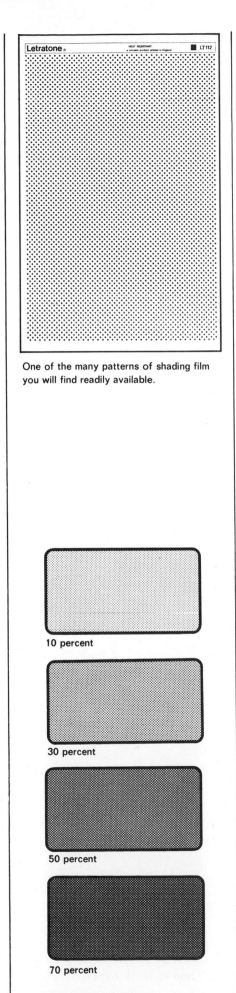

One of the many patterns of shading film you will find readily available.

10 percent

30 percent

50 percent

70 percent

Samples of tint percentages.

the dots. It is like mixing a white paint into a jar of a solid color. The admixture of white turns the color into a lighter tone — the more white, the lighter the tone (or tint). Conventionally, tints are described in multiples of ten, with one hundred representing the solid color and zero being pure white.

To Apply the Tint

Shading film (as it is called) comes in sheets that are transparent and adhesive, bearing a printed pattern of dots (or lines and textures). They are available at most art supply shops under trade names such as Letraset, Craftint, Zipatone, and others. You can select the pattern you wish from a free catalog sheet.

Apply a section of this film sheet over the area you wish to tone. Use enough to extend beyond the edges of your area. Press it lightly to the surface of the board, smoothing it down with a straight edge. Then, with an X-Acto knife, or blade, cut the exact shape of the area you wish to tone. The surplus will strip off easily and can be reused. Now place a clean sheet of paper over the film and burnish the film lightly yet firmly.

Check the film for dirt particles and air bubbles. Where air bubbles exist, prick them carefully with a sharp point and press down again. In the case of dirt or scratches, do not waste time cleaning but remove the film and replace it with a new section.

To Order a Color Tint

You may wish to avoid the work entailed in applying the shading film. With a blue pencil, you can indicate on the mechanical itself, or on an overlay sheet of transparent tissue, the area you wish to tint. Each area on the mechanical that is to receive the tint must be carefully and legibly marked as to the percentage of tint and also the color of ink to be used (e.g., 80 percent blue, 30 percent black).

Your platemaker will then apply the appropriate tint by using the Ben Day process, which is the universally used method for obtaining tints. The technicalities involved need not concern you. Your printer will supply you with the range of patterns and tints available.

Bear in mind that screen tints will usually print about 10 percent darker than the sample. And, of course, there will be a charge for the work of applying the tint by the platemaker.

Here are just some of the shading film patterns available in sheet form from Letraset, one of the largest makers. They can be used on illustrations and backgrounds — as shown on the following pages — to obtain varied textures and other effects easily and simply by mounting over a photo or illustration. Obtain a catalog from your art supply dealer for a full range as well as explanation on uses.

Varied Uses of Shading Film

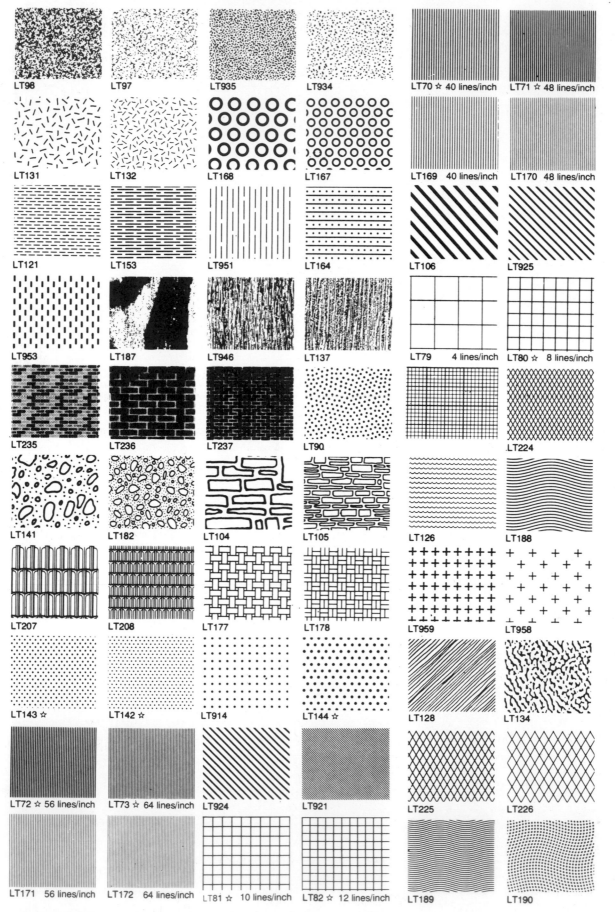

LT98 LT97 LT935 LT934 LT70 ☆ 40 lines/inch LT71 ☆ 48 lines/inch

LT131 LT132 LT168 LT167 LT169 40 lines/inch LT170 48 lines/inch

LT121 LT153 LT951 LT164 LT106 LT925

LT953 LT187 LT946 LT137 LT79 4 lines/inch LT80 ☆ 8 lines/inch

LT235 LT236 LT237 LT90 LT224

LT141 LT182 LT104 LT105 LT126 LT188

LT207 LT208 LT177 LT178 LT959 LT958

LT143 ☆ LT142 ☆ LT914 LT144 ☆ LT128 LT134

LT72 ☆ 56 lines/inch LT73 ☆ 64 lines/inch LT924 LT921 LT225 LT226

LT171 56 lines/inch LT172 64 lines/inch LT81 ☆ 10 lines/inch LT82 ☆ 12 lines/inch LT189 LT190

A sampling of shading film patterns available from Letraset.

140

Instantex is a unique dry transfer system for adding shading and tonal effects to artwork and illustrations. Instantex can be rubbed down onto any art surface simply by pressure from the cap of a ball-point pen. The artwork can be reproduced immediately.

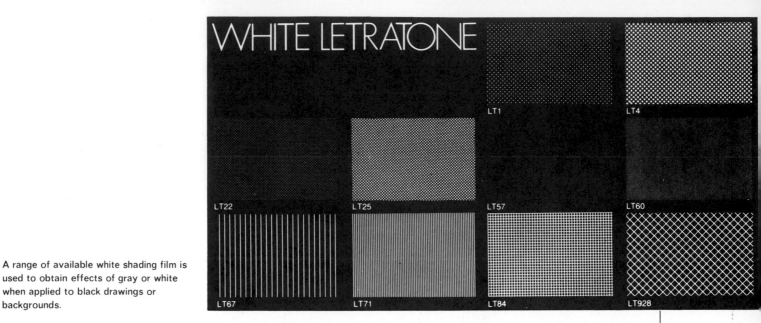

A range of available white shading film is used to obtain effects of gray or white when applied to black drawings or backgrounds.

The Use and Effects of White Dot Shading Film

Original line drawing.

Shading film applied with overlap.

Shading film trimmed and cut as desired.

Development of a Reverse Linecut Ad

Black dot shading film applied as wide border gives three-tone effect while printing in one color, black on white.

The original positive.

The negative photostat.

The positive has white shading film over
the letters.

The negative has white shading film over
the entire background.

Lacking any illustration and heavy with copy, this powerful two-column ad was developed as shown on the following pages.

The layout is designed.

All type is ordered in positive form and pasteup of each unit is carefully made according to layout.

A negative (white on black)...

...and a positive (black on white) photostat are made.

Following the layout, the white panels are cut to size and then pasted on the negative photostat.

White shading film is mounted over the entire area, then trimmed and cut away from white panels. The mechanical is now ready for the photoengraver.

THE PHOTOSTAT

No single item used by the advertising artist has more varied uses than the photostat. It is absolutely essential that anyone remotely concerned with the production of advertising matter become fully aware of its multiple functions as well as how to order it and how to use it.

Photostats are a fast and economical way of duplicating any part of a layout either same size, enlarged, or reduced to specific needs. They are available in white on black (negative) or in black on white (positive). For linecut work, which means solid tone, they are print ready as finished art. For halftones, which means photographs or wash drawings, they are useful for showing appearance and positioning of an illustration on a layout or a mechanical. Also, as line drawings they may be colored with paints, inks, or dyes.

How to Order and Use

The photostat machine will enlarge the original up to twice its size or reduce it to half its size in a single step. This first step produces the negative, which is usually white on black (if the original is black on white). This negative is made on heavy white paper and may be used as is, if you can use the reverse of the original color. If larger than double the original size is wanted, or smaller than half, the negative can be made in two steps. However, if you start with a 5" x 10" (13 x 25 cm) original and you want it four times this size, or 20" x 40" (51 x 102 cm), you can order the first negative twice up, or 10" x 20" (25 x 51 cm), and then have this negative doubled up to give you the 20" x 40" (51 x 102 cm) you want. This will save time and money.

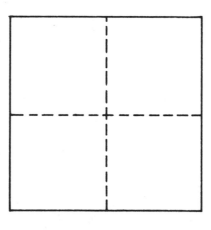
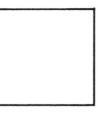

If you need a photostat four times the size of the original, order the first negative "twice up," and then have the negative "doubled up."

The first step in making any photostat results in the reverse of your original — be it black on white or white on black — and this is your negative. The second step will reverse the negative. Hence a black on white duplicate requires two steps. The second one is called the positive. In indicating size wanted, you draw a line with a two-headed arrow along one side of your original (safely away from any part of it) and mark the size wanted, in inches and fractions, along the stem of the arrow. For same size duplicate, mark "s/s."

Photostats are made on several kinds of paper, each serving a purpose. A matte finish is the least expensive, and is suitable for appearance on a layout or mechanical. This finish is not intended for reproduction. The

Photostats can be made of positives or negatives. Initially, a positive will be turned into a negative; a negative to a positive.

146

As photostats can be reduced or enlarged, you will need to indicate on your original the size of the photostat you require.

Smile all the way

← — 5″ pos. — →

most widely used photostat is made on glossy paper. Here the black has maximum density and contrast and is perfectly suited for reproduction by the photoengraver's camera. Also, if you intend to color the stat (for layout work), ask for PMC paper, which takes paint without wrinkling.

Should you have a drawing of a figure facing one way, and you want it to face the opposite way, ask that your original be "flopped." It is then photographed in a mirror to produce a reverse image.

Costs of stats are based on the size of paper used. You may, therefore, assemble more than one unit for a single photostat. If the paper used does not exceed 8½″ x 11″ (22 x 28 cm) you will be charged for one job.

Costs can be minimized by ordering one photostat of multiple sections and then cutting out each section as required.

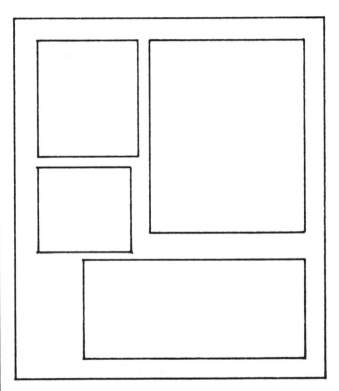

THE OVERLAY

This is a most important adjunct and aid in setting up the mechanical. It permits the handling and positioning of units that cannot be put together for one reason or another.

To provide instructions for the platemaker concerning any unit, it is enough to mount a sheet of tissue over the mechanical, with tape along the top edge. You may then outline any part of the pasteup with blue pencil and make notations within the area you are outlining.

When any part of the mechanical that is to be printed cannot be mounted on the base sheet of illustration board, a transparent sheet of clear acetate

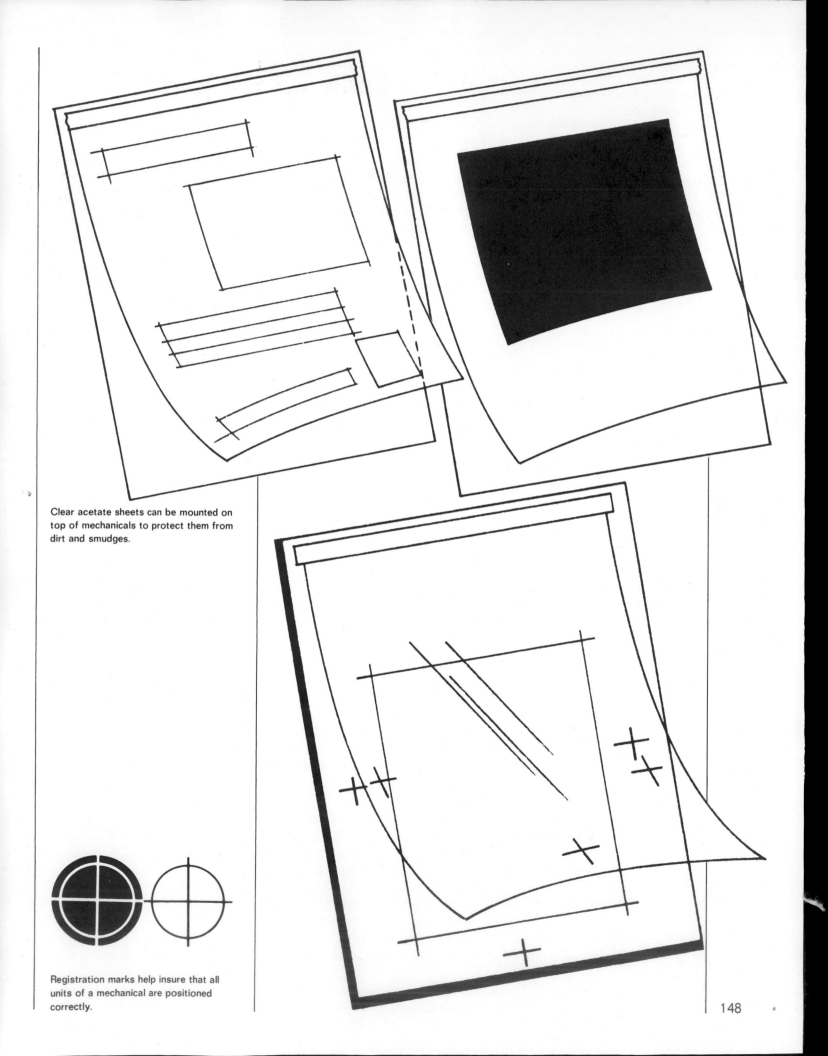

Clear acetate sheets can be mounted on
top of mechanicals to protect them from
dirt and smudges.

Registration marks help insure that all
units of a mechanical are positioned
correctly.

148

is mounted over the mechanical and taped along the top. This permits the use of ink when necessary and it then becomes an integral part of the job.

Also, when a solid black area is to be printed and it cannot be done on the base, you can mount a self-adhesive red film (obtainable in most art supply stores) on the clear acetate. It is easily cut to shape after mounting with a blade or knife, thus assuring sharp corners. This red film will photograph as black, and being transparent permits easy positioning, with registration marks both on the board and the acetate.

Other uses of overlays are:

To define shaded areas when this cannot be done on the board itself.

For location of alternate copy when parts of the copy are to be changed.

To prepare combination line and halftone plates where each must be handled separately.

To position art or type that will be overprinted or dropped out of a background.

REGISTRATION MARKS

The register or accurate positioning of an element on the mechanical is a critical factor at all times, and especially so in any color printing.

It is a way to make certain that all units are positioned correctly with relationship to each other according to the original layout.

This is done by drawing thin cross lines about ¾" (2 cm) long on three sides of the base mechanical, at least 1" (2.5 cm) away from any element of the job.

After an overlay is taped in position, these marks are drawn on the overlay, matching closely with those on the base. The registration marks on succeeding overlays should be a little shorter than the preceding one (less than ¾" [2 cm]). Preprinted registration marks on clear tape may be obtained, or they can easily be made with any fine point pen, using acetate ink.

CROPPING AN ILLUSTRATION

The effectiveness of an illustration can be greatly increased by selecting that portion of the picture that will best suit your purpose and by eliminating the rest. Use of the cropper's L's (as described under Illustration) will give the greatest variety of possible shots to choose from in any easy and rapid manner. Take the time to select a shot that will be dramatic and interesting. Remember that no matter how small the portion you choose, you may enlarge it to provide a dramatic closeup.

Once you make your choice of the shot, you can outline the area by running a white grease pencil inside the edges of the opening (for photo). If you are cropping a drawing or wash painting, you may do the same with a pointed soft pencil. In either case, you will mask out the outside area, cutting an opening in a piece of bristol board, same size, and cement it over the picture.

Cropping can provide increased impact.

SCALING AN ILLUSTRATION

A simple procedure for scaling the proportions of an illustration.

Your photo or drawing, cropped and shaped to suit you, now must be reduced or enlarged to fit the layout measurement. You may do this by indicating, on a tissue overlay, the measurement of the longest side as you wish it. Your engraver can take it from there.

But this may result in a proportion that is different from your layout. If you wish to see exactly how it will appear on the mechanical, you may scale it up or down by drawing a diagonal through the corners and carrying this line out to the height you want. Then, draw a perpendicular and horizontal line through this point and you will have an accurate scaled-up area of the cropped illustration. You may then decide to alter the cropping to suit the layout, or to be closer to it.

If the foregoing has been observed, your mechanical should now be ready for the platemaker. You are not ready to take it to him until you have checked it for errors, which are *very* expensive to correct. Check off the following items:

Have you proofread all copy?

Is everything really clean?

Are sizes and measurements exact?

Is there proper alignment of units?

Are blacks really black?

Does the type need retouching?

Is halftone copy clearly positioned and indicated?

Are all screen tints carefully marked for percentage and color?

Is all overlay material accurately registered?

Are you leaving anything to chance or guesswork?

THE HALFTONE PLATE

If your design or layout calls for the use of a photograph or a black-and-white painting (usually a watercolor wash), you will require a different kind of printing plate, called a halftone, which contains a full range of tones between black and white.

Bear in mind that everything printed in a newspaper is printed with black ink only. No gray ink is used. Yet, it is possible to give the effect of gray in any number of shades or tones from very light to near black. This effect is an optical illusion caused by a breakdown of a black area into a series of black dots. Dots are large where the picture is dark and gradually become imperceptible where the picture is light. This, briefly, is the basis for all printing that requires reproduction of a photograph or painting in a single color.

The halftone plate contains a full range of tones between black and white.

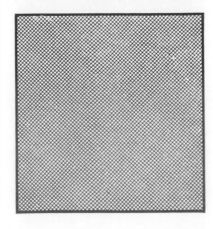

A photograph (upper left) that was photoengraved without the use of a halftone screen. Just two tones — black and white — were obtained. The same photograph (upper right) was photoengraved with the use of a halftone screen. This faithfully reproduces the original in all tones and shades. Lower left shows the halftone screen that enabled the photoengraver to reproduce accurately all the tones of the copy from the deepest black to absolute white.

The halftone method is by far the most widely used means of producing, on a plate, illustrations that have a continuous tone. It represents a branch of photoengraving but differs from the making of a simple linecut in that a screen is placed between the camera and the object to be photographed. This screen consists of fine black lines ruled at right angles to each other on clear glass. The number of lines to the square inch on the screen varies, and the one used depends on the grade of paper.

For newspaper work a sixty-five line screen will usually give good results. If a finer screen is used, the porous nature of the paper makes the ink dots run together and blot. Some publications require a certain screen, ranging up to 200 lines for the finest kind of printing. Your platemaker will use the proper screen if you tell him the paper you will be printing on. Also, some jobs will require use of a combination plate for best results. Until you are knowledgeable in this area, it is best to be guided by your printer or photoengraver.

If the photograph or painting to be reproduced is the size called for in your layout, you have only to indicate the area on the mechanical, with a red pencil line, and write "strip in original art," then key the picture with a letter corresponding to the one you will put on the mechanical.

If your illustration is not the exact size needed — and it seldom is unless specifically ordered — then you must make it fit. In doing so, you will make use of the opportunity to crop it.

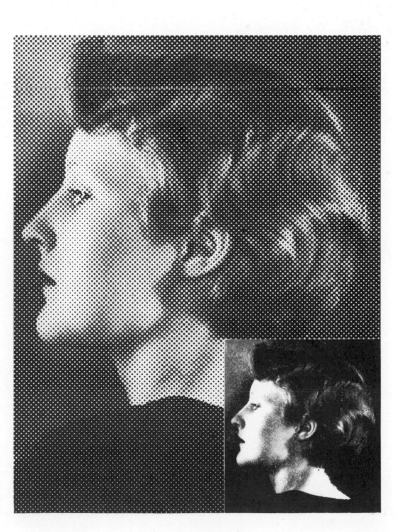

The halftone at the lower right was made with a 110-line screen. In the larger illustration this same halftone has been enlarged until it equals a thirty-line screen. When it is held at a normal reading distance the lines of dots are readily seen. When held at a greater distance of about eight feet, the dots blend together, thus giving the impression of a continuous tone.

153

55 line

85 line

110 line

The same illustration is reproduced here by means of three different screens. The accuracy of the detail is increased by finer screens.

To print a halftone background with solid type in black or white, use a combination plate.

The Combination Plate

We have seen where the preparation for printing a linecut plate (no gradations of tone) is a simple matter of assembling all the units on a single board, in clear solid black, no matter the eventual color printing. From this mechanical pasteup, the photoengraver has no problem in converting the pastup into a plate which is then used for the actual printing.

Similarly, we know that any illustration with tones ranging from light to dark requires a halftone plate, made by photographing our illustration

through a glass screen, obtaining a positive print, and then converting the print into a linecut plate, where the dot patterns will give the illusion of being a continuous tone photograph.

However, some ads will call for a halftone background with solid type in back or white. Here, we have what is called a combination plate, part of which is the halftone illustration and another part, the copy, made in line. This is true of jobs where a black or white type is needed over the halftone background.

If the type were to be mounted directly on the illustration (by means of an overlay), and then shot through a screen as a halftone, the dot pattern would make the edges of the letters appear ragged. To avoid this, we prepare our mechanical first with the background as a halftone, and then with a transparent overlay, applying the type over the halftone. We can now shoot the entire thing as a linecut. The halftone will retain the dot pattern while the type is shot clear and solid with non-ragged edges.

This involves the preparation of the mechanical for the combination plate, in two stages; first, the halftone print, and then the black or white type mounted on overlays over the halftone.

If your platemaker is supplied with all the necessary units, with a layout showing what you want, he will take it from there.

Ballinger, Raymond A. **Art & Reproduction**. New York: Van Nostrand Reinhold, 1977.

———— **Layout and Graphic Design**. New York: Van Nostrand Reinhold, 1970.

Cardamone, Tom. **Mechanical Color Separation Skills for the Commercial Artist.** New York: Van Nostrand Reinhold, 1979.

Craig, James. **Designing with Type.** New York: Van Nostrand Reinhold, 1980.

———— **Production for the Graphic Designer.** New York: Watson-Guptill Publications, 1974.

Gray, Bill. **Studio Tips for Artists and Graphic Designers.** New York: Van Nostrand Reinhold, 1976.

———— **More Studio Tips for Artists and Graphic Designers.** New York: Van Nostrand Reinhold, 1978.

———— **Lettering Tips for Artists, Graphic Designers and Calligraphers.** New York: Van Nostrand Reinhold, 1980.

King, Jean C. and Esposito, Tony. **The Designer's Guide to Text Type.** New York: Van Nostrand Reinhold, 1980.

Rice, Don. **Animals: A Picture Sourcebook.** New York: Van Nostrand Reinhold, 1979.

———— **Birds: A Picture Sourcebook.** New York: Van Nostrand Reinhold, 1980.

———— **Fishes, Reptiles and Amphibians: A Picture Sourcebook.** New York: Van Nostrand Reinhold, 1981.

Rice, Stanley. **Type-Caster: Universal Copyfitting.** New York: Van Nostrand Reinhold, 1980.

Rosen, Ben. **Type and Typography, Revised Edition.** New York: Van Nostrand Reinhold, 1976.

Silver, Gerald A. **Graphic Layout and Design.** New York: Van Nostrand Reinhold, 1981.

Spectre, Peter and Putz, George. **Marine Art Clipbook.** New York: Van Nostrand Reinhold, 1980.

Stone, Bernard and Eckstein, Arthur. **Preparing Art for Printing.** New York: Van Nostrand Reinhold, 1965.

Switkin, Abraham. **Hand Lettering Today.** New York: Harper & Row, 1976.

Szabo, Marc. **Drawing File for Architects, Illustrators, and Designers.** New York: Van Nostrand Reinhold, 1976.

Type Specimen Book. New York: Van Nostrand Reinhold, 1974.

Typony. **Etcetera: Graphic Devices.** New York: Van Nostrand Reinhold, 1980.

Van Uchelen, Rod. **Paste-Up.** New York: Van Nostrand Reinhold, 1976.

———— **Say It With Pictures.** New York: Van Nostrand Reinhold, 1976.

Volk and Huxley. **Mergenthaler VIP Typeface Catalog,** Volumes 1 and 2. New York: Van Nostrand Reinhold, 1980.

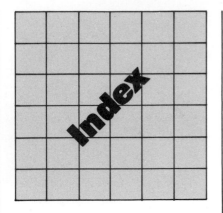